TURKEY

TITLES IN THE MODERN NATIONS OF THE WORLD SERIES INCLUDE:

Afghanistan	Japan
Australia	Jordan
Austria	Kenya
Brazil	Lebanon
Cambodia	Mexico
Canada	Nigeria
China	Norway
Cuba	Pakistan
Czech Republic	Peru
Egypt	Poland
England	Russia
Ethiopia	Saudi Arabia
France	Scotland
Germany	Somalia
Greece	South Africa
Haiti	South Korea
Hungary	Spain
India	Sweden
Iran	Switzerland
Iraq	Taiwan
Ireland	Thailand
Israel	Turkey
Italy	United States
	Vietnam

MODERN
NATIONS
—OF THE—
WORLD

TURKEY

BY CHRIS EBOCH

**LUCENT
BOOKS®**

THOMSON

GALE

San Diego • Detroit • New York • San Francisco • Cleveland
New Haven, Conn. • Waterville, Maine • London • Munich

THOMSON
━━━━━✦━━━━━™
GALE

LIBRARY OF CONGRESS CATALOGING-IN-PUBLICATION DATA

Eboch, Chris
    Turkey / by Chris Eboch.
    v. cm. — (Modern nations of the world)
    Includes bibliographical references and index.
    Contents: Where continents collide—The passing of empires—The republic—Daily life—
Arts and entertainment—Today's challenges
        ISBN 1-59018-122-0
        1. Turkey—Juvenile Literature. [1. Turkey.] I. Title. II. Series.
        DR417.4. E26 2003
        956.1—dc21

                                                                                2002011052

Printed in the United States of America

CONTENTS

INTRODUCTION   6
  Crossroads of Cultures

CHAPTER ONE   9
  Where Continents Collide

CHAPTER TWO   22
  The Passing of Empires

CHAPTER THREE   39
  The Republic

CHAPTER FOUR   56
  Daily Life

CHAPTER FIVE   69
  Arts and Entertainment

CHAPTER SIX   83
  Today's Challenges

  Facts About Turkey   97
  Notes   99
  Chronology   102
  For Further Reading   104
  Works Consulted   106
  Index   108
  Picture Credits   112
  About the Author   112

Introduction

Crossroads of Cultures

For over three thousand years Turkey has been a meeting place of cultures. Sometimes these meetings have been violent struggles for control, but in the end they created a vibrant and varied society with some of the most remarkable historical and archeological sites in the world.

The Turks call their country the "Land of Civilizations." Sitting at the point where Europe, Asia, and Africa are closest to each other, Turkey has seen wave after wave of migration. The country was a natural path for trade routes, but also offered easy access to invaders. Cities toppled in turn to the Persians, Macedonians, Romans, Seljuks, Mongols, and Ottomans. As guidebook authors Dana Facaros and Michael Pauls say, "If we learned in school that early history belonged almost entirely to Egypt and the Fertile Crescent, it is only because chance led the archaeologists there first. The mountains and plains of Anatolia can . . . also stake their claim as one of the birthplaces of civilization."[1]

In the sixteenth century, Turkey was the center of one of the world's greatest empires. The Ottoman sultans controlled lands that extended into southeast Europe, western Asia, and northern Africa. They brought Islam to millions, and their lavish lifestyle created awe throughout Europe. Yet over time the Ottoman Empire weakened and shrank. By the start of the twentieth century, European powers were ready to take over and divide Turkey.

The Turks had other ideas, however. Led by one great visionary, Mustafa Kemal, Turkey demanded its place in the modern world. It also made a dramatic shift—from traditional Middle Eastern society, ruled by a dictator and governed by Islamic law, to a Western-style secular democracy. Within a decade the country changed completely. Unfortunately, Turkey could not keep up with its own growth. Schools could not educate enough architects and engineers. Small farmers sold their land and moved to the cities searching for

work. The poor resented the rich, and devout Muslims hated the government's laws against religion. Protests sometimes turned into riots.

A nineteenth-century painting depicts the fall of Constantinople. Turkey has a rich but often violent history.

TODAY AND TOMORROW

In recent years the country has stabilized. Turkey is dedicated to becoming a modern nation with a strong economy, but is still struggling to catch up with its European neighbors.

In remote areas, people still live much as their ancestors did. Sod-roofed huts, horse-drawn carts, and wandering shepherds are still common. Meanwhile, today's modern cities contain office buildings, apartments, and trendy suburbs. In the cities young people may study business, medicine, or engineering. Art, music, and literature often blend ancient traditions with modern innovations.

Turkey comes from a cultural tradition that is Islamic and Middle Eastern. Yet the country has looked to Europe for examples of economic development. Today life in Turkey overlays modern political, scientific, and economic advances on a foundation of traditional Turkish culture and religion. Most Turks want to join the modern world without losing their unique heritage. If Turkey succeeds in taking a strong place among the nations of the world, it will carry on its position as a crossroads, a meeting place of cultures, bridging the gap between the countries and cultures of Europe and the Middle East.

Where Continents Collide

Turkey's position on the border of two continents has defined the landscape. The vast Asian and European continents collide in Turkey. A third continent, Africa, lies just across the Mediterranean Sea. These continents are attached to plates in the earth's crust that drift apart or slide together. If a plate moves with a sudden jolt, earthquakes shake the land. As the continents push against each other, the earth erupts into mountain ranges. The many mountain ranges that cross Turkey are a result of these three great continents rubbing together. Other mountains were built up by volcanic eruptions, a result of the movement of plates exposing the earth's molten core. Turkey's position at the meeting point of continents created the country's geographic features, a flat central plain surrounded by mountain ranges and ringed by rugged coasts.

Location and Boundaries

Turkey's present borders were established in 1923. The country is roughly rectangular and occupies a little over three hundred thousand square miles. That makes it bigger than Texas, and larger than any European country except Russia. The greatest east-to-west distance is just over one thousand miles, while the greatest north-to-south distance is a little under five hundred miles.

Turkey is mainly defined by the coastline of the Anatolian Peninsula of Asia, also known as Asia Minor. This piece of the Asian continent has the Black Sea to the north, the Aegean to the west, and the Mediterranean to the south. Despite having water on three sides, Turkey shares borders with eight other countries. On the Asian continent, Turkey touches six countries: Georgia, Armenia, and a tiny corner of Azerbaijan to the northeast; and the Middle Eastern countries of Iran,

Iraq, and Syria to the southeast. Three percent of Turkey is on the European continent, on the Balkan Peninsula, bordering Greece and Bulgaria to the northwest. The Sea of Marmara divides this section from the Anatolian Peninsula.

TURKISH THRACE

The small corner of Turkey that lies on the European continent is called Turkish Thrace. This area is covered with fertile, rolling hills. About a quarter of the region is farmland, on which crops such as wine grapes, figs, olives, and melons are grown. The climate is mild, with temperatures seldom below freezing or above eighty-five degrees Fahrenheit. The area is humid, however, with a rainy season that runs from December to March.

Turkey's borders entirely enclose the Sea of Marmara, a body of water that divides Turkish Thrace in Europe from the rest of the country on the Asian continent. Called "the smallest sea in the world," Marmara is forty-eight miles across at its widest point. At each end it narrows to channels just over a mile wide. Marmara is linked to the Black Sea in the north through the Bosphorus Strait, and to the Aegean Sea in the south through a channel called the Dardanelles. For thousands of years this has been an important trade route, the fastest path between the Mediterranean region and the countries north of the Black Sea.

Though quiet and pastoral now, Turkish Thrace has seen many battles as people fought over control of this trade route. The most recent conflict was the Battle of Gallipoli during World War I. Britain tried to conquer Thrace so they could keep a sea route open to their ally, Russia. Hundreds of thousands of soldiers died before the Turks won the battle. The area is now the Gelibolu Peninsula Historical National Park, where foreign and Turkish soldiers are buried in thirty-one cemeteries.

ISTANBUL

Turkey's largest city, Istanbul, takes advantage of its position on the Sea of Marmara. Like Turkey itself, Istanbul straddles both Europe and Asia. The city is divided by water into three districts: Stamboul, Beyoglu, and Uskudar. Stamboul, the oldest part of the city, lies on the European shore in Turkish Thrace. Surrounded on three sides by water, this hilly peninsula was easily defended and has a safe natural harbor, fertile land, and a mild climate.

For these reasons, the city was the capital of three successive empires, the Roman, Byzantine, and Ottoman. More than 120 emperors and sultans reigned from this city over a period of nearly sixteen hundred years. Originally called Byzantium, the city was renamed Constantinople in A.D. 330. After A.D. 1453 it was called Istanbul, from a Greek phrase meaning "to the city." Istanbul still holds hundreds of historic sites reflecting the civilizations that called it home, from Roman mosaics to Byzantine churches to Ottoman mosques.

The city grew under Ottoman rule, adding settlements on nearby shores. A long inlet known as the Golden Horn separates Stamboul from Beyoglu, a district of offices, shops, and suburbs. The third district, Uskudar, lies across the Bosporus Strait on the Asian shore. This is an area of modern housing and industry. The three districts are now connected by bridges and ferries. Though no longer the capital city, Istanbul remains the economic and social center of Turkey, with at least 7 million inhabitants.

Istanbul, located on the Sea of Marmara, is the largest city in Turkey.

THE AEGEAN COAST

From Istanbul, the Sea of Marmara flows south through the Dardanelles to the Aegean Sea. The Aegean coastline is rugged, with rocky cliffs and many inlets. Rivers feed rich farmland between the steep hills. Although on the Asian continent, Turkey's Aegean coast was first settled by European Greeks beginning five thousand years ago. Many villages hold the remains of ancient temples and theaters among more recent buildings. Halfway down the coast lies Izmir, an economic center of industry and trade. Izmir is Turkey's second largest port and third largest population center (after Istanbul and Ankara) with about three million residents. South of Izmir, the modern city of Bergama sits near the ancient site of Pergamum, a port city that prospered in the second century B.C. under Macedonian rule. The people of Pergamum invented parchment, a paper made of goatskin, and built a famous library. But in the first century B.C. the Roman leader Marc Antony gave the entire collection to the Egyptian Queen Cleopatra as a sign of his love for her. The two hundred thousand manuscripts joined the Alexandria library in Egypt, where they were later destroyed in a fire. Today tourists flock to the Pergamum ruins, where they climb a one thousand-foot hill to the remains of palaces, temples, and marketplaces.

The valley below Pergamum holds another popular tourist attraction, the Asklepion. This famous medical center, which reached the height of its popularity in the second century A.D., treated disease with mud baths, fasting, concerts, and doses of sacred water. According to travel writer Lynn Levine, "Hours of therapy probed the meaning of the previous night's dreams; patients believed dreams recounted a visit by the god Asklepios, who held the key to curing the illness."[2]

South of Bergama lies the biblical city of Ephesus, or Efes in Turkish. Greeks founded the city in the eleventh century B.C., and it later became Roman. The Christian Saints Paul and John reportedly preached there in the first century A.D. Streets paved with marble lead to partially reconstructed buildings, such as a stadium, a twenty-five-thousand-seat theater, and a

The biblical city of Ephesus houses many ruins, including a stadium, and theater, and this library.

library. Archeologists are still excavating noble houses, many several stories high and decorated with intricate mosaics or painted murals.

THE MEDITERRANEAN COAST

From the Aegean, Turkey's Mediterranean coast winds east along the Mediterranean Sea. The Italian merchant Marco Polo visited the coast in the thirteenth century. Europeans still flock to this popular vacation area, known as the Turkish Riviera. Resorts and nightclubs are clustered near endless beaches. Archeological sites and natural beauty also draw visitors. Flamingos nest in the river valleys, and sea turtles lay their eggs on the beaches in May. The long, gently curving coastline has mild, rainy winters and long, hot summers. On the fertile strips between mountains and sea, farmers grow olives, citrus fruit, grapes, figs, vegetables, and cotton.

Inland, the region is mountainous and wooded. For centuries, the mountains have provided marble and cedar wood for building. Landslides are common on steep slopes, so agriculture is limited to the valleys, lower hills, and along the coast. Most of the people also live along the coast, where they make their living mainly from the fishing and tourism.

THE BLACK SEA COAST

The Black Sea region is cooler and rainier than the Aegean and Mediterranean coasts. This is the wettest part of Turkey, with over one hundred inches of rain a year. Perhaps for this reason, it has been less popular with both ancient settlers and modern tourists. Still, Greek legend associates the coast with the mythical women warriors called Amazons, the hero Hercules, and the voyage of Jason and the Argonauts. Several coastal cities were also stops on the Silk Road, an ancient trade route between China and Rome. Merchants from Genoa, Italy, settled the area from the thirteenth to fifteenth centuries and built castles that still remain.

Although the coast offers few good natural harbors, several artificial harbors have been built. Today the Black Sea coast has several trading ports and is a favorite spot for fishing, boating, and other water sports. The sea is home to fish such as sturgeon, while monk seals haunt caves along the shore.

Beyond the thin strip of coast, high mountain ranges rise steeply, with thick forests of pine, poplar, and oak. The

TRAVEL BY CAMEL

Long before cars, caravans traveled through the Middle East. Some trade routes stretched thousands of miles, much of it through empty desert. These roads had three-foot-wide paved tracks for horsemen, with unpaved paths on either side for walkers and farm animals. The traffic included trade caravans of camels and donkeys piled high with baggage, army convoys, religious pilgrims visiting holy sites, and shepherds with their flocks.

During the Ottoman Empire, sultans ordered many caravan stops built, especially during the thirteenth century. They were spaced twenty-five to thirty miles apart, a day's travel, on major trade routes. These buildings, called caravansaries or khans, welcomed every traveler to stay free for up to three days. The government paid for these early hotels in order to promote trade by giving merchants a safe place to spend the night.

Some khans were simple stone buildings, with an open courtyard for the caravan animals. Travelers would camp on a waist-high ledge that ran around the courtyard, sleeping on carpets with their saddles for pillows. They would cook their meals at one of the fireplaces there.

In cities, the merchants paid for their lodgings. These larger khans might offer travelers private rooms, covered halls for the animals, storage rooms, a mosque, a blacksmith, a coffee shop, and a bathing room where men could wash off the dust of the road. According to Raphaela Lewis, author of *Everyday Life in Ottoman Turkey*, these khans also offered "an evening meal, usually a large wooden platter holding a dish of pilaf made of cracked wheat or barley and a little stewed meat, with loaves of bread and sometimes a comb of honey." In most cities, a market surrounded the khan. Shops lined each side of the covered alleys—saddle-makers and sweetshops, jewelers and grocers, barbers and butchers. Along with a place to rest, the khan offered everything else a traveler might need or want.

mountains, with their many lakes, rivers, and waterfalls, are popular with Turkish hikers, trout fishers, white-water rafters, and skiers. In the valleys and lower mountain slopes, farmers grow cherries, hazelnuts, tea, tobacco, flowers, and corn. Steel mills and coal mining are also important to the economy in this area.

CENTRAL ANATOLIA

The many coastal mountain ranges of Turkey make a ring around the Central Anatolian Plateau. The plateau slopes upward toward the east, where the mountain ranges meet at a high point of 12,848 feet at Mt. Erciyes.

Archeological remains show that people built villages in Central Anatolia ten thousand years ago, making these the oldest settlements in Turkey. Later, trade routes passed through Anatolia, and so did waves of invaders. Greeks, Persians, Romans, and Christian Crusaders came from the west, and Turkish-speaking nomads came from Central Asia. But few people stayed, and today much of this vast land is empty.

Central Anatolia seldom sees rain, and sometimes suffers severe droughts. Winters are cool and windy, summers hot and dry. The land has a burnt yellow color broken by patches of green, without much variation in the plant species. Jacky ter Horst-Meijer writes, "The area is largely deforested and, with the exception of the extremely dry middle region, consists of an endless grassy plain. In the neighbourhood of villages, where the land is irrigated, wheat and barley are the

A fortress sits high atop the Turkish capital. In the centuries since the fortress was built, Ankara has expanded into a vibrant, modern city.

main agricultural products. On the steppes, which are closely-cropped due to grazing, there is only room for poplars and tenacious thistle species among the agricultural crops and the olive orchards."[3]

The Plateau contains scattered towns, but the most important city today is Ankara, the Turkish capital. Ankara was settled at least three thousand years ago. Legend says that Amazons founded the city, but more likely the settlers were Hittites, an ancient people from Asia Minor and the Middle East. Ankara still has a small section of old narrow streets and mud houses, surrounding a ninth-century fortress on top of a hill. Ankara became Turkey's capital in 1923. Since then the modern city has expanded, and is now home to 4 million people. Ankara is a lively city with great museums, art and music festivals, and prestigious universities.

CAPPADOCIA

In the middle of the vast Central Anatolian Plateau lies a triangle of land known as Cappadocia, which means "land of beautiful horses," named for the fine horses raised there more than two thousand years ago. Millions of years ago, erupting volcanoes deposited layers of lava, ash, and mud over the surrounding countryside. Wind and rain eroded this soft rock into spectacular gorges, cones, and tall cylinders known as "fairy chimneys." The soft colors of the rock—pink, yellow, gray, cream, and shades of brown—add to the enchanted look.

Because the region has few trees to use as building material, people traditionally dug their homes out of the soft rock. Valley cliffs are pocked with living quarters, generally single rectangular rooms. Even stables were carved into the rock for domestic animals. Although the area never held many people, thousands of empty cave houses remain, because the rock walls can survive for centuries.

Beginning about four thousand years ago, the locals dug out underground cities for extra protection against invaders. Over two hundred of these cities are known; about forty of them go at least three levels deep. Some could hold over twenty thousand people. The small, dark rooms had air shafts but little light, so these were probably not permanent homes, but rather offered temporary escape from invaders. The tunnels could be blocked off by massive stone wheels.

Today tourists flock to the region, many staying in cave hotels outfitted with electricity and plumbing. Visitors wander among pink-and-tan rock hills, exploring cave churches dating from A.D. 900 to 1200, when the area was a refuge for early Christians. In the fourth century, Saint Basil developed the practice of monasticism, the belief that people should live in small groups devoted to poverty, labor, and spirituality. Many monks and nuns gathered in Cappadocia over the centuries, where they carved churches and living quarters out of the rock. One six-story convent housed up to three hundred nuns. In the convent dining room, even the long table and benches are carved from the stone. The churches are painted with Christian symbols and scenes from the lives of the saints. Saint George, born in Cappadocia and considered a local hero, is often shown slaying a dragon.

Only a few cave homes are still in use. In 1952, the government declared the entire village of Zelve unsafe due to earthquake risks and moved the people to more modern houses. Now most people live in small towns with conveniences such as running water. Yet in some villages women still bake their bread in outdoor ovens, and potters use many of the same techniques as the ancient Hittites when they make dishes and cups for tourists to buy.

THE EASTERN HIGHLANDS

The Eastern Highlands is a mountainous region that slopes up to seven thousand feet near the Iranian border. About one hundred mountain peaks rise over 10,000 feet. Turkey's highest mountain, Mount Ararat, soars 17,011 feet—over three miles—above sea level. An extinct volcano, Ararat rises in a cone from the flat surrounding plain. Marco Polo described it in his journals: "In the heart of Greater Armenia is a very high mountain, shaped like a cup, on which Noah's ark is said to have rested, whence it is called the Mountain of Noah's Ark. It is so broad and long that it takes more than two days to go around it. On the summit the snow lies so deep all the year round that no one can ever climb it."[4]

The melting snows of Ararat turn the surrounding land into a bog in spring, but the government has been draining many areas for farming. Less than 10 percent of the Eastern Highlands is cultivated so far. Summers are mild, but winters are very cold, with temperatures as low as minus forty de-

This cave church dates from medieval times in Cappadocia, when the region was a refuge for early Christians.

grees Fahrenheit. Snow, up to forty feet in a year, blankets much of the land for four months. A few ski resorts take advantage of the cold and snow.

The Eastern Highlands lie to the east of the mountain ranges that surround the Central Anatolian Plateau. This part of Turkey is farthest from modern Europe, both physically and culturally. The majority of the people here are ethnic Kurds, traditional nomads who wandered freely throughout the Middle East. Wild horses run the plains and shepherds roam the plateau with huge dogs to defend their sheep from wolves and bears. Many people still live in sod-roofed huts and travel in horse-drawn carts. Villagers tend to be more traditional and religious than city dwellers in the west.

THE FERTILE CRESCENT

The Eastern Highlands region is the source of the Tigris and Euphrates Rivers, which empty into the Persian Gulf. The rivers contain a triangle of land that extends into Syria and Iraq. This is the Fertile Crescent, known as the cradle of civilization. Many advanced ancient cultures developed here, starting with the Sumerians about fifty-five hundred years ago. From the Fertile Crescent people spread throughout Asia and Europe. According to Facaros and Pauls, "This quarter of Turkey lies just outside the boundary of the known and familiar, where mere geography evaporates into myth along the banks of the Tigris and Euphrates . . . and the ghosts of numberless dead civilizations rise up to spook you from their mouldering ruins."[5]

The part of the Fertile Crescent that lies within Turkey is a rolling plateau with mountains to the west, north, and east. Many cities and towns rest on the site of ancient settlements, perhaps dating back to the Hittites before 1200 B.C. Two ancient cities associated with the Bible sit near the border with Syria. Pilgrims visit Sanliurfa (formerly Urfa), where supposedly Job lived and the prophet Abraham was born in a cave. Locals believe that these dry hills were the site of the Garden of Eden, where the first humans lived. Though drier than it used to be, parts of the Fertile Crescent are still fertile. Grain farming is common, and to the west farmers cultivate olives, pistachio nuts, and wine grapes. The Fertile Crescent is now the hottest part of Turkey, with summer temperatures often reaching 110 degrees Fahrenheit.

NORTH CYPRUS

One other region should be mentioned in connection with Turkey. Although no other country recognizes the claim, Turkey considers the northern third of the nation of Cyprus, an island in the Mediterranean Sea, to be the "Turkish Republic of North Cyprus." Of the 175,000 residents, about 40,000 are immigrants from the Turkish mainland. Most of the others are Turkish Cypriot (ethnic Turks born in Cyprus). Turkish is the official language and the Turkish lira is the official currency.

Cyprus has hot, dry summers and a long rainy season from October to March. A rocky mountain range along the coast encloses a flat, treeless plain. The main natural resource is agricultural land, and most people make a living by farming and raising livestock. The mineral copper was named for Cyprus because the island was the main source of copper for the ancient world. Copper is still mined there, but mining is no longer an important industry.

Turkey as a whole contains a great variety of geography: rugged mountains, high plateaus, fertile valleys, barren rock outcroppings, and sunny beaches. People have left their mark on the country's landscape, too, in the form of ancient ruins, quaint villages, and bustling modern cities. The Asian and European continents collide in Turkey with an explosion of natural features.

2

THE PASSING OF EMPIRES

With its position between Europe and Asia, Turkey has been a crossroads of cultures. Travelers entering Turkey from each continent provided thousands of years of settlement, conflict, and changing society. Warriors, refugees, and immigrants came alternately from the east and from the west. Some groups stayed only briefly, while others made Turkey their home and imposed their language and culture on the local inhabitants. A few empires lasted hundreds of years, but even the strongest eventually fell to the next wave of invaders. As a meeting place of cultures, Turkey has been influenced successively by these empires from the east and the west.

THE FIRST EMPIRE

People have lived in Turkey from the dawn of humankind. Starting six hundred thousand years ago, Old Stone Age tribes lived in caves, hunted, and gathered wild foods. During the New Stone Age period, from 8000 to 5000 B.C., people settled in villages. They lived in mud-brick houses, farmed grain, raised cattle for food, and built religious shrines painted with human and animal figures.

By 2000 B.C. new tribes began migrating into Turkey from the north and east. Some of these tribes took over local towns and built large city-states. The most powerful group, the Hittites, created an empire that lasted from about 1650 to 1200 B.C. They conquered most of what is now Turkey and forced the local people to adopt their language and culture. The Hittites built a large capital city, Hattusa, in central Anatolia. Hattusa was a walled city with a fortress, temples, and government buildings. Archeologists have learned about the Hittites from the records they left behind: thousands of clay tablets with cuneiform, or wedge-shaped, writing. The Hittite empire collapsed around 1200 B.C. and split into many independent city-states.

INVADERS FROM WEST AND EAST

Greek colonists settled along Turkey's western coast starting around 1000 B.C. Their settlements, at first poor farming villages, grew into strong cities. But once again invaders came from the east, from what is now Iran. Persian armies marched through Turkey to the Aegean coast during the sixth century B.C. Persian governors then ruled the Greek cities along Turkey's coast for about two hundred years and remained in control of central Turkey even longer.

Alexander the Great, pictured here in a seventeenth-century painting, invaded Turkey during the fourth century B.C.

HISTORIC ISTANBUL

For centuries Istanbul has been famous for both its natural beauty and the splendor of its buildings. In his story "The Rose of Istamboul," the Ottoman writer Bahloal Dana described the "heaped miracle of Istamboul . . . a mountain of minarets and rainbow domes, lofting into the illimitable turquoise of the Eastern night. . . . When Nature and Man set hands to the same canvas what, with the aid of Allah, could they not achieve?"

Most historic sites are clustered in the old city, Stamboul. Aya Sofya (St. Sophia) was built as a church by Constantine the Great and rebuilt by Justinian in the sixth century. When the church was finished, Justinian said, "Glory to God who has deigned to let me finish so great a work. O Solomon, I have outdone thee!" Two years later the church dome collapsed after an earthquake. The Aya Sofya was rebuilt many times after such damage. In 1204, European Crusaders looted the church and stole many valuable works of art. When Sultan Mehmed II conquered Istanbul in 1453, he converted St. Sophia into a mosque. The building is now a museum with walls decorated in a mix of Byzantine mosaics and Islamic calligraphy art.

Novelist Mary Lee Settle described her visit in *Turkish Reflections*. "Thousands of people from all over the world visit Aya Sofya every day, as they have done since it was built. But now, instead of the voices of Goths and Latins, and rough Galatians, and traders from Cathay, instead of the shaggy skin trousers of the Scythians, the togas of the Romans from the west, the white robes of the Arab tribes, the stiff gold-laden caftans of the Byzantines, the silk shifts of the traders from China, there are English voices, and German, and French, and Japanese, tourists dressed in clothes that seem in modern times to be all alike, a world of jeans and T-shirts . . . ."

Another popular tourist site that is still used for worship is the nearby Sultanahmet Mosque, or Blue Mosque, which gets its nickname from the color of the twenty thousand tiles that decorate the interior. Sultan Ahmet I, who had the mosque built in the early 1600s, wanted to create something even more glorious than the Aya Sofya. Many say he succeeded with this beautiful mosque, famous for its six slender towers, or minarets.

A new power then rose in the West. Alexander the Great succeeded in uniting his home region of Macedonia with the Greek states, which had formerly been independent. He then turned his armies eastward. They swept through Turkey in 334 B.C. Alexander defeated the Persians and founded many cities along his path of conquest. Greek army veterans settled in them, once again bringing Greek culture into Turkey. Alexander and his generals tried to force all the local people to adopt the Greek religion, though most people compromised with a mix of their old customs and the new.

The Greek cities along the Aegean flourished. Wealthy people lived in comfortable houses with running water and decorative mosaic floors. Many cities built theaters, museums, and concert halls. The government was an early form of democracy, with decisions made by an assembly of the people. Not everyone benefited, however, because many people were slaves and women had few rights.

This new rule did not last long. Alexander died of a fever in 323 B.C. at age thirty-three. After his death, his generals divided up his empire. They split Turkey into several independent kingdoms and fought each other for power. Other groups continued to invade, including Gauls, a Celtic people from what is today France, who settled in central Turkey.

REUNITING WITH THE WEST

In the century after Alexander's death, Greek power faded. As Roman armies conquered land throughout the Mediterranean region, Rome became the new center of the world. The great city of Pergamum, along Turkey's western coast, allied itself with the Roman Empire for protection against other invaders. When the last king of Pergamum died in 133 B.C., he left a will that gave his empire to the Roman Republic. With this foothold in Turkey, the Roman Empire began taking over the rest of Asia Minor. By 66 B.C. Rome's rule extended throughout the Middle East.

In the third century A.D., the Roman Empire split into independent provinces. One of these, the Eastern Roman Empire, had its capital in Constantinople, today called Istanbul. By A.D. 476, the Western Roman Empire had been conquered by Germanic invaders, but the Eastern Roman Empire lasted for another thousand years. During this era, known as the Byzantine period, the Eastern Roman Empire was governed by the principles of Roman law, the official language was Greek, and most people were Christian. At its peak, the Eastern Roman Empire ruled parts of southern Europe, southwestern Asia, and northern Africa.

Like every empire before it, this one fell. Slavs from the north, Persians from the east, and Arabs from the southeast conquered some of its territories. Mongols, Russians, and Bulgars attacked. The Byzantine royal family fought over who would be emperor. Finally the weakened empire crumbled. Though Byzantine emperors ruled Constantinople until the fifteenth century, they began to lose the rest of their territory.

THE FIRST SULTANS

Turkey gained much of its present character starting in the eleventh century with the invasion of the Seljuks. These nomads from Central Asia are the original Turks. They came from Outer Mongolia and are related to other nomadic Asian groups such as the Huns and Mongols. Most of these tribes followed shamanistic religions with many gods. Then in the seventh century, the Seljuks encountered Islam, a religion based on the teachings of the Arab prophet Muhammad. Over the next few hundred years, most Turks converted to Islam.

Islam united its followers, even if they were of different tribes or races. According to historian Roderic Davison, "Islam served as a new bond among all those Turks who professed it. It was not simply a method of worship or a narrow religious creed, but a way of life. . . . Law and state, society and culture, were built on and permeated by Islam."[6]

Islamic Seljuk warriors took control of neighboring Iraq and Iran in the eleventh century. They began raiding Anatolia with the help of another Turkish tribe, the Turkoman. In 1071 the Seljuks destroyed the Byzantine forces at a battle near Lake Van in eastern Turkey. The Central Plateau lay defenseless, and Turkish armies swept across Anatolia. By 1078 they were getting close to Constantinople.

The Byzantine Emperor Alexius called Christian Crusaders to his aid. In 1097 the First Crusade recaptured about a third of Anatolia. The Seljuks kept control of the Central Plateau, where their rulers, called sultans, flourished for over a century. They built roads, stone bridges, and a network of inns known as caravansaries. The remains of their mosques, religious schools, and fortresses are still scattered across central Anatolia. New Turkish tribal groups also migrated into Anatolia from Central Asia. As they mixed with the local population, more people converted to Islam. Many Jews and Christians still lived in Turkey, but Greek influence faded as Turkish culture took root.

Once again the invaders became the invaded. Mongols, led by a grandson of the famous warrior Genghis Khan, defeated the Seljuks in 1243. The Mongols collected tribute and allowed the Seljuks to continue governing, but the Seljuk state weakened, with power divided between many small regions ruled by Turkish princes.

THE OTTOMAN EMPIRE

New leadership came from an unexpected place—a small principality, or emirate, in northwestern Anatolia. Davison writes, "It was by no means the biggest or strongest of the emirates, and it must be a matter of surprise that not only the greatest Turkish-ruled state, but also the greatest Islamic empire of history, grew from this tiny state."[7] Legend says that the Turkoman leader Osman led troops of horsemen into western Turkey, helped the Seljuk win an important battle, and was rewarded with the emirate nearest to Constantinople. In the 1290s Osman founded the Ottoman Empire. His descendants expanded the empire through the conquest of Christian Byzantine lands, and by buying Islamic Turkish lands or acquiring them through marriage. By 1400, Osman's

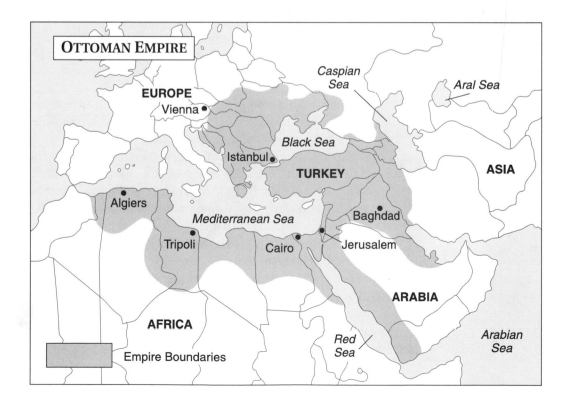

During the fifteenth-century, a Mongol named Tamerlane (center, atop elephant) invaded Anatolia to challenge the Ottoman's power there.

grandson, Bayezid, ruled a kingdom from the Danube River in Bulgaria to the Euphrates. He seemed poised to become the world's most powerful leader.

Then a new challenger stepped forward. The Mongol Tamerlane, a military genius, had already conquered much of Iran and central Asia. In 1402 he destroyed Bayezid's forces in Anatolia. Tamerlane did not want to rule Anatolia; he just wanted to keep anyone else from getting too powerful there. He split the Ottoman Empire back into several principalities, some ruled by Bayezid's sons.

A period of civil war followed as Bayezid's sons fought for control of the Ottoman realm. Other principalities struggled to remain independent, while European neighbors backed whomever was weakest, in an attempt to keep the strong from getting stronger. Finally Bayezid's son Mehmed emerged the victor. He defeated his brothers and reunited the Ottoman Empire by 1413.

THE GROWTH OF POWER

Mehmed succeeded partly because none of his enemies, in Anatolia or in Europe, had the strength to challenge him for long. European rulers worried about the Ottomans but were too busy fighting each other to join forces against them. Some of the conquered people may even have preferred Turkish rule to the repressive Byzantines. The Turks generally allowed freedom of religion, and people of any race or class could become successful merchants, artisans, or administrators.

The Ottoman sultans also had a strong, organized army, with Turkoman cavalry and slave soldiers. Warfare was considered holy, because it brought Islamic rule to more people. A fifteenth-century Ottoman chronicler described the religious warriors called Ghazis: "A Ghazi is the instrument of the religion of Allah, a servant of God who purifies the earth from the filth of polytheism; the Ghazi is the sword of God."[8]

Soldiers were recruited from among the conquered Christian peasants. Boys between the ages of eight and twenty were taken from their villages and trained at the palace school. According to Davison, "Here, following a curriculum broader than that of the traditional Muslim school, they learned Turkish, Arabic, and Persian; studied the Koran [Muslim holy book]; absorbed some history, mathematics, and music; became proficient in horsemanship and weaponry; underwent rigorous physical training; learned a craft or trade; and learned etiquette as well."[9]

Once they were separated from their families, villages, and previous ways of life, these soldiers owed loyalty only to the sultan. They could own property and could rise to positions of wealth and power. Some even became grand vizier, second in command after the sultan. But because they were slaves, their children could not inherit their money or rank. This system rewarded people based on their own abilities, and prevented any family from establishing a powerful dynasty that could threaten the sultan.

With these soldiers, the Ottoman sultans continued to expand their kingdom. Sultan Mehmed II captured Constantinople in 1453 and made it the Ottoman capital, renamed Istanbul. The Ottomans pushed into the edge of Greece, Palestine, Egypt, and Arabia. In Anatolia, Turkish rule was firmly established. According to historian Douglas A. Howard, "By the time Sultan Mehmed II took Istanbul, most of Anatolia had been under Muslim Turkish rule for more than four centuries. Even the still heavily Greek and Christian Aegean coastal regions had become accustomed to the authority of Muslim sultanates after more than 150 years."[10] The Ottoman Empire was now a major world power.

INTERNAL ADVANCES

Mehmed II rebuilt Istanbul as a majestic political, economic, and cultural center. He brought merchants and artists from throughout his empire to work in the city, and ordered the building of a great mosque, a bazaar, baths, roads, and inns for caravan travelers. He called learned men to his court: poets, historians, artists, and philosophers. A Spanish traveler of the time wrote that the Turks were "a noble people, much given to truth. . . . They are very merry and benevolent, and of good conversation, so much so that in those parts, when one speaks of virtue, it is sufficient to say that anyone is like a Turk."[11]

Judges enforced traditional Islamic law. Religious organizations supported schools, hospitals, soup kitchens, and mosques, as well as public fountains and gardens, markets, baths, libraries, and inns. Trade flourished, with spices from India and Egypt, silk from Iran, and wool cloth from Italy. Anatolia produced and traded rugs, furs, beeswax, musk, and cloth of cotton, silk, or mohair.

In accordance with Muslim law, non-Muslim people had to pay a special tax to the government. Still, their rights were protected. Each religious community—in Turkey mainly Jews, Greek Orthodox Christians, and Armenian Christians—could arrange its own educational and legal system. Non-Muslims were also prohibited from holding top government posts, but race and background did not matter. Anyone who converted to Islam had a chance at advancement. For example, black slaves from Africa held many important positions in the royal court. The primary restriction on rights was based on gender. As in the earlier Byzantine era, women rarely left their homes and they wore veils outside. They had few rights and seldom took part in public or political life.

SULEIMAN THE MAGNIFICENT

The Ottoman Empire reached its political and cultural height during the reign of the Sultan Suleiman, from 1520 to

1566. He was known to the west as Suleiman the Magnificent for the richness of his court, but his own people called him Suleiman the Lawgiver, for his fair legislation. By the end of his life the Ottoman Empire was the ruling power on the Mediterranean Sea and controlled much of the Balkans, northern Africa, and the Middle East. In a letter to the king of France, Suleiman described himself: "I who am the sultan of sultans, the sovereign of sovereigns, the distributor of crowns to the monarchs of the surface of the globe, the shadow of God on earth. . . . "[12]

Suleiman personally led his army of fifty thousand soldiers into thirteen brutal wars, while in between he wrote poetry and studied the works of the famous Greek philosopher Aristotle.

A sixteenth-century painting depicts Mehmed II's capture of Constantinople in 1453; Mehmed II renamed the city Istanbul and made it the capital of the Ottoman Empire.

Under the rule of Suleiman the Magnificent (pictured right), the Ottoman Empire reached the peak of its political and cultural achievements.

On Fridays, the Muslim holy day, Suleiman dressed in a fur-trimmed robe and a turban decorated with diamonds and peacock feathers. He rode a white horse past throngs of people on his way to worship at Aya Sofya mosque.

The sultan's harem, or family quarters, contained his mother, concubines, young children, and female servants. Sultans did not marry, but the first four concubines to bear the sultan a son became "wives" and their sons stood in line for the throne. Suleiman had three hundred concubines, slave women from all over the empire. He had a son with one concubine, but soon after that he got a new slave from Russia, a girl known as Roxelana. Suleiman fell in love with her, consulted her on government matters, and eventually astonished the empire by marrying her. Roxelana influenced Suleiman so much that she convinced him to murder his eldest son, the popular heir to the throne. Roxelana died before Suleiman, but she had attained her goal. Her son Selim became sultan when Suleiman died in 1566 after forty-five years of rule.

THE LONG DECLINE

Unfortunately, Selim was a lazy drunkard unfit to rule. With his reign, the Ottoman Empire began to deteriorate. The first ten Ottoman sultans, from Osman to Suleiman, led their own armies into battle, were skilled politicians, and were interested in art, literature, and history. But according to writer Noel Barber, "The twenty-five sultans who followed Suleiman were, almost without exception, totally lacking in any of the qualities needed to rule."[13]

Selim died after only eight years on the throne. Drunk on wine, he slipped while climbing into the bath and broke his skull. The hundred years after Selim's death are known as "the reign of favored women." While royal men thought only of pleasure, the harem women fought for power and manipulated weak sultans from behind the scenes. The harem gained extra power by a change in the rules of succession. Previously, when a new sultan took the throne he killed all his brothers, so none could challenge him. This practice was meant to keep the government stable and avoid civil war. After 1600, boys in line for the throne were not killed, but they were kept prisoner in the harem, the women's quarters. After living their whole lives in this "gilded cage," they ascended to the throne with no experience in government, warfare, or even public life.

The bureaucracy grew into an unwieldy mass of departments and officials. Corruption was common at all levels, and people now gained power through bribery or favoritism. Grand viziers were frequently executed at a sultan's whim. The soldiers demanded more and more benefits. They rebelled several times, sometimes killing court officials. The population had doubled in less than a century, causing poverty and food shortages, and the peasants of eastern Anatolia revolted in protest.

Some sultans and their advisors tried to modernize the country, but they made limited progress. Large landowners, regional governors, and the military kept a tight grip on their power and the luxuries it brought them. Any sultan who tried to make dramatic changes was overthrown. While European nations made advances in technology and industry, the Ottoman Empire stagnated.

THE "SICK MAN OF EUROPE"

For centuries, religious and ethnic minorities had lived peacefully with their Turkish Muslim neighbors. That changed in the nineteenth century with the decay of the Ottoman Empire and the misrule by its sultans. Minorities were mistreated and sometimes killed. Ethnic nationalism—the desire for an independent homeland—grew into open rebellion. According to travel writer Tom Brosnahan, "The subject peoples of the Ottoman Empire rose in revolt, one after another, often with the direct encouragement and assistance of the European powers who coveted parts of the sultan's vast domains."[14] For example, Greek Christians began a rebellion in 1824, envisioning a return to the days when Greece ruled much of the ancient world. With naval help from Britain, France, and Russia, Greece won its independence in 1830, though with a smaller territory than the Greeks had desired.

Despite its weakness, the Ottoman Empire remained important. Whoever controlled the region around Constantinople influenced trade on the Mediterranean and Black Seas, as well as between Europe and Asia. European powers—Britain, France, Germany, Italy, Russia, and the Austro-Hungarian Empire—waited hungrily for the Ottoman Empire to collapse, so they could expand their own empires. The Turks ignored the signs of trouble, believing their Empire would last forever. The Turkish diplomat Fuad Pasha wryly told a Western associate, "Our state is the strongest state. For you are trying to cause its collapse from the outside, and we from the inside, but still it does not collapse."[15]

Sultans began to borrow money from European countries, supposedly to modernize. In reality, much of the money went to build ornate palaces and pay for lavish parties. As a result, Turkey grew economically dependent on France, England, and Germany, and when the Ottoman Empire went bankrupt in 1875, those countries demanded reforms.

In 1876, Sultan Abdul Hamit II took the throne. His grand vizier designed a constitution and ruling parliament in an attempt to reform the government. Though the sultan still held

LIFE IN THE HAREM

The end of the Stamboul peninsula, the oldest part of Istanbul, contains the grounds of Topkapi Palace. The residence of sultans from the fifteenth through nineteenth centuries, Topkapi Palace was a fortress with homes, offices, libraries, kitchens, and gardens. Five thousand people lived and worked in this majestic city-within-a-city; over one thousand servants worked in the largest kitchens in the world. Noel Barber, author of *The Sultans*, writes, "This was a hidden world of golden domes and pointed minarets reaching for the sky like manicured fingers; of dark cypress groves hiding kiosks, or villas, their walls of marble, glittering mosaics or exquisite tiles; of artificial lakes and pleasure gardens, of the mingled scents of herbs and fruit trees and roses, of an imperative silence broken only by the tinkling of scores of fountains. . . . no court in Europe was its equal."

The harem, or family quarters, lay within the palace. A sultan's family consisted of hundreds of slave women, either bought from their parents, captured in war, or given as gifts. In his *Istanbul* guidebook, Tom Brosnahan describes their life. "Upon entering the Harem, the girls would be schooled in Islam and Turkish culture and language, the arts of make-up, dress, comportment, music, reading and writing, embroidery and dancing. They then entered a meritocracy, first as ladies-in-waiting to the sultan's concubines and children, then to the sultan's mother and finally, if they were the best, to the sultan himself." The sultan's mother was the most powerful woman in the harem, followed by those concubines who had borne him a son. They lived in great luxury. Most of the other women lived dull lives as servants, crowded several to a small room where they slept on the floor. They might never even see the sultan, and were never allowed outside the harem. Eunuchs, usually black men sent as slaves from Egypt, guarded the women.

Today, the palace contains museums with exhibits of silver, crystal, ceramics, costumes, jewels, manuscripts, and ancient artifacts. One museum holds relics of the Prophet Muhammad, including hairs from his beard, a tooth, and soil from his grave.

most of the power, the constitution guaranteed personal liberty for everyone. Pressure from Europe forced Hamit to agree, but he dissolved the parliament in 1878. Once again the sultan ruled with absolute power. Hamit modernized the country by building schools, railways, and telegraph lines, but he refused democratic reforms. He used spies and secret police to control the country through fear.

THE SULTAN GOES TOO FAR

Hamit's tactics were not enough to discourage rebellion. Serbia, Bulgaria, and Romania gained independence in 1878.

Hundreds of thousands of Muslim refugees flooded into Anatolia from those countries. Rebellions continued in Armenia, Crete, and Macedonia. Hamit blamed the European powers for encouraging the rebellions. "By taking Greece and Romania," he said, they "cut off the feet of the Turkish state. By taking Bulgaria, Serbia and Egypt they cut off our hands. Now by stirring up trouble among the Armenians they are getting close to our vital organs and want to cut out our intestines. This is the beginning of mass destruction. We must defend ourselves at all costs."[16]

As part of his defense, Hamit ordered the slaughter of Armenians throughout the Empire. At least one hundred thousand men, women, and children died. Some were killed

Sultan Abdul Hamit II rides in an Istanbul park. While Hamit II modernized Turkey by building schools, railways, and telegraph lines, he refused to implement democratic reforms.

BATHS AND TOILETS

Hygiene was very important to the Romans, and they are noted for the plumbing designs used in their baths and toilets. Private homes had toilets either near the entrance, near the kitchen, or in an alley behind the house. Most cities also had public latrines in the city center, near busy markets or theaters. The ancient Roman city of Ephesus, on Turkey's Aegean Coast, had a public latrine that could seat 40 people at a time on marble benches. Water flowed through drainage channels or pipes that carried the waste away. An open shaft in the middle of the room let in light and fresh air. Many bathrooms had murals on the walls or mosaic tile designs on the floor.

Today most Turkish hotels and many tourist sites have modern, Western-style toilets. But some public restrooms have Eastern-style toilets, where the user squats over a porcelain- or cement-lined hole in the floor.

Bathing was also important to the Romans, and public bathhouses played a part in social life. People met friends and did business in rooms decorated with mosaics and marble statues. Some towns drew on natural warm mineral springs for their water. Otherwise, aquaducts supplied the water, which was heated by a furnace. Terracotta pipes circulated hot air through the walls to keep the room warm and steamy.

Islam puts great value on personal cleanliness, so the Ottoman Turks embraced public baths, or *hamams*, and built hundreds just in Istanbul. Like the Roman bathhouses, they too are public but men and women bathe separately, either in different baths or at the same *hamam* on different days. These *hamams* are designed more like saunas, with warm, steamy rooms for relaxing. The washing rooms contain small marble basins with hot and cold running water. Bathers splash themselves with water instead of soaking in it. They can lie on a warmed marble table for a vigorous massage, or even have an attendant wash and shampoo them. Afterward, the bather takes a nap or relaxes with coffee, tea, or a cold drink.

outright; others died from starvation, disease, or exhaustion during months-long forced marches as they were expelled from Turkey. Europeans and Turks alike were outraged, Barber claims. "Significantly, many of [Hamit's] subjects joined the outside world in their condemnation of the Sultan's creed of extermination. During the three years of intermittent massacres thousands of pious Moslems, sickened by the debauchery, sheltered their Armenian neighbours."[17] Thereafter, Abdul Hamit became known as "Abdul the Damned."

Some Turks, bitter and angry over the decay of the country, had been forming secret political societies. Now they came out into the open. The Committee of Union and Progress, often called the Young Turk movement, promoted democracy with the motto "Liberty, Justice, Equality, Fraternity." Backed by the army, they forced the sultan to restore the constitution in 1908. "A brief Indian summer of the Ottoman Empire ensued," claim journalists Nicole and Hugh Pope, "with genuine scenes of brotherhood between the various ethnic and religious communities."[18] The new elected parliament contained 147 Turks, 60 Arabs, 27 Albanians, 26 Greeks, 14 Armenians, 10 Slavs, and 2 Jews.

A country cannot change overnight, however. A counterrevolution attempted to restore the sultan, but failed. Hamit was exiled, his harem slaves sent back to their mountain villages, and his weak brother Mahomet V was put on the throne. Mahomet V reigned merely as a figurehead with little power, while the Young Turks tried to build a new government. Territories that had long been ruled by the Ottoman Empire took advantage of the disorder to declare their independence. The great days of the Empire were at an end.

THE REPUBLIC

In the twentieth century, Turkey's leaders tried to build a new nation by moving away from the country's Arab past toward a European future. Most Turks welcomed the changes taking place in the early 1900s. The country would suffer for many more years, however, while the new government tried to sort out its identity and ideals. Political groups squabbled over who would control the Empire, what policies they should follow, and how much they should Westernize or preserve traditional ways.

THE NEW LEADERS

The Young Turks took many steps toward modernization. Their most important decision was to put aside the Islamic law that had ruled the country for so many centuries. Instead they modeled their government on Western-style democracy, where religion is officially separate from government. The Young Turks hired European advisors to help update Turkey's laws, financial system, military, and agriculture. Schools became more secular (nonreligious). Educational and public opportunities increased for women; some even began wearing European clothing. The press had more freedom to report the truth.

The Young Turks found their idealistic dreams hard to achieve, however. They had planned an empire on the principle of "Ottomanization," where people of all nationalities would be equal and loyal to the Ottoman government. But the provinces continued to rebel; they preferred to become their own independent countries. The Young Turks tried to control the situation by repressing differences. They shifted to an ideal of "Turkism," where everyone would be equal because they were the same—specifically, like the Muslim Turks. They forbade political groups based on nationality or

During the early twentieth century, Talaat, Cemal, and Enver (pictured from left to right) controlled Turkey.

ethnicity. They even tried to force everyone in the Empire to speak Turkish. Government leaders spent most of their time fighting for their own political survival, which sometimes involved rigging elections or killing opponents.

By 1913 three Young Turks controlled the Empire: Talaat, Cemal, and Enver (most Turks used only one name at the time). Talaat was a huge, friendly man who lived simply but governed ruthlessly as Minister of the Interior. Cemal was a hard-drinking gambler with a black beard and piercing eyes. As Military Governor of Constantinople and Minister of Marine, he did not hesitate to use assassination as a political weapon. Enver was young and handsome, with an upturned mustache. He was a popular hero after leading the rebel soldiers against Sultan Hamid, but his charm hid vanity and cruelty. He took over the position of War Minister by force in 1911, married the sultan's daughter, and moved into an ornate palace. Together these leaders drove through harsh and sometimes violent reforms.

THE START OF WAR

The struggling country needed foreign aid to modernize, but Turkey did not have many allies. Britain and France did not take the new government seriously, and Russia was an old enemy. Germany was their strongest friend. German banks invested in Turkish electricity, mining, agriculture, and transportation. Not everyone welcomed the Germans, but Enver saw Germany as an ideal modern country. He invited thousands of Germans to train the Turkish army.

Then on June 28, 1914, the Archduke Franz Ferdinand, heir to the Austrian and Hungarian thrones, was assassinated at Sarajevo in Bosnia. This event set off World War I. The "Triple Alliance" of Austria-Hungary, Germany, and Italy fought together against the "Entente Powers" of Russia, France, and England, although Italy later changed sides. Enver signed a secret pact with Germany that said that Turkey would remain neutral in the war, but they would close the Bosporus to international shipping, thereby cutting Russia off from its Western allies.

Turkey did not stay neutral for long. The government had previously ordered two warships from England. Turkish sailors were already in England and the first ship was ready to sail. Then England refused to send the ships, instead taking them for its own navy. The people of Turkey were furious. When Germany offered to replace the warships, Enver agreed.

Talaat argued, "We want nothing more than to be left out of war, and have a period of peace in which we can build for the future."[19] But Enver, hoping to take back some of the land Turkey had lost in recent years, sent warships against Russia in the Black Sea. Almost by accident, Turkey found itself at war with the Entente Powers of England, France, and Russia.

"THE ARMENIAN PROBLEM"

Turkey faced fighting from within as well as from outside enemies. For fifteen hundred years Christian Armenians had lived in the northeast part of Asia Minor bordering Russia. During the war, many of them allied themselves with Russia in the hope that Russia would help Armenia become independent. Thousands of Armenians fought in the Russian army, while others carried out guerrilla attacks within Turkey. The Ottoman government ordered all Armenians deported to Syria and Iraq. Deportation soon turned to killing.

Armenian women were raped or kidnapped by mountain tribesmen, with the encouragement of the government. Armenian men were tortured and shot. One group of eighteen thousand people, mostly women and children, were forced to march for seventy days across the desert. They were robbed of every article of clothing, repeatedly beaten, and went for

ETHNIC GROUPS

About 66 million people live in Turkey. The majority are ethnic Turks, whose ancestors came from central Asia. About 10 million Kurds also live in Turkey. Most are Muslim and have features similar to Turks, but their language and culture are different.

Turkey had millions of ethnic Greeks during the Ottoman Empire. Most returned to Greece during WWI and the Turkish War of Independence. After the war, Turkey and Greece agreed to a population exchange that sent many more Greeks to the home of their ancestors. Now fewer than 100,000 ethnic Greeks live in Turkey, most in Istanbul.

Turkey has an estimated twenty-four thousand Jews, most of them also living in Istanbul. In the sixteenth century, many Jews fled Spain because they were persecuted by the Spanish Inquisition. The Ottoman Empire welcomed these Jews for their knowledge of European science and economics. Jews have had a strong presence in Turkey ever since, though many emigrated to Israel after the founding of the Jewish state in 1948.

Armenians lived in eastern Anatolia for thousands of years. In the last century, however, most were killed or forced to leave. Istanbul still has a small Armenian population, with its own churches and schools, but few other Armenians live in Turkey today.

---

days without food or water. Only 150 survived the march. Most historians estimate that between 800,000 and 1 million Armenians were killed or died of disease or starvation. Turkish politicians have denied responsibility, and people still argue about who exactly ordered the killings. Talaat admitted some guilt in a 1918 speech, when he said, "During a war that is about the life or death of a country, we could show no indulgence to those who endangered the security of the army . . . many innocent people were undeniably sacrificed."[20]

GALLIPOLI

While the Armenians were being slaughtered in the east, western Turkey faced a different battle. Entente leaders hoped to help Russia and drive Turkey out of the war by taking control of the Dardanelles, the strait south of Istanbul. Warships tried to enter the strait, but underwater mines sank three ships and forced the others to retreat. The retreat gave

Turkey time to strengthen its defenses. The Entente commanders decided to try a land campaign next. Britain chose to attack the Gallipoli Peninsula, a rocky, barren land along the north of the straits.

Britain should have had an easy battle, but the British made foolish decisions because they believed the Turks were

In 1915, General Sir Ian Hamilton and his British troops tried to capture Turkey's Gallipoli Peninsula.

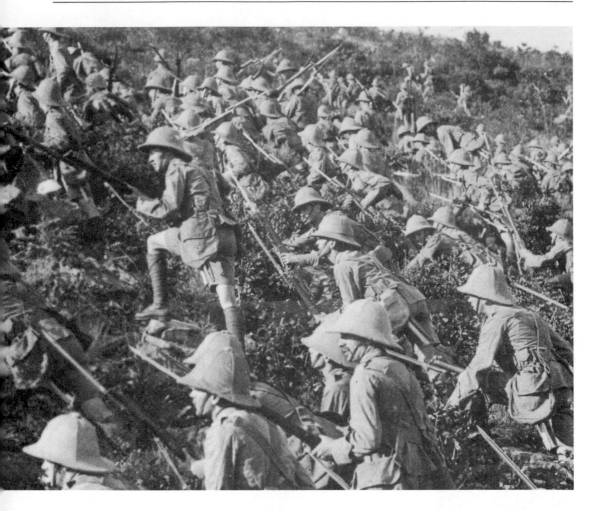

British soldiers invade Gallipoli. The battle with Turkish troops was a disastrous defeat for the British.

inferior and could never stand up to the British forces. General Sir Ian Hamilton, the British officer in command, split his soldiers into five groups to land in different spots. He assumed the Turks would be confused and would not fight back until his troops were in place.

On three beaches, the Entente forces landed without trouble. But instead of pushing inland, two groups stayed on the beach and waited for orders that never came. The Turks took advantage of the delay to bring in reinforcements and dig defensive trenches. Only one group, the renowned Australian–New Zealand Army Corps, known as ANZAC, tried to advance. A small group of Turks led by an army colonel named Mustafa Kemal kept the ANZAC soldiers pinned down on the open slopes and beaches. At two other beaches, the British soldiers struggled to even reach shore. Fewer than one hundred Turks defended those two beaches, but the Brits had to land in a hail of machine gun fire. Britain lost twenty thousand soldiers there in one day.

Instead of the quick victory they had planned, the Entente soldiers faced long and bloody trench warfare. They attacked and retreated again and again. Both sides suffered weary stretches of hiding in trenches in harsh weather, including torrential rains and snowstorms. In eight long months, the Entente powers recorded 265,000 soldiers wounded, killed, or missing. The Turks suffered an estimated 300,000 casualties. Half of all the soldiers who fought at Gallipoli died.

The British had failed so miserably that many English officials lost their jobs. General Hamilton was replaced by General Sir Charles Munro, who quickly decided that nothing more could be accomplished at Gallipoli. He led an evacuation, and so the battle ended on January 9, 1916. The battle had one lasting effect that would direct the future of Turkey: Mustafa Kemal became a Turkish hero for his brave leadership.

THE MISERY OF WAR

Turkey's success did not extend to other areas. The Arab provinces rebelled, and by 1918 Palestine, Syria, and Iraq had escaped Ottoman rule. The Empire suffered an even greater spiritual loss with the cities of Mecca and Medina, in what is today Saudi Arabia. The Ottoman Empire no longer controlled Islam's most holy cities. Russia conquered the eastern half of Anatolia, where nearly eighty-five thousand Turkish soldiers died, mostly from the cold.

The Turkish army didn't have enough uniforms or shoes, and medical treatment barely existed. At least 580,000 Ottoman soldiers died in World War I, over half of them from disease. Civilian Turks also suffered from disease and famine. About one quarter of the population died during or soon after the war, including 2,500,000 Muslims, at least 800,000 Armenians, and about 300,000 Greeks.

Turkey's allies were also suffering, and they finally asked for a truce to end the war. The Turkish citizens had had enough. Enver and Talaat fled Istanbul on a German boat. Two weeks later, the Ottoman government surrendered to Britain. The Young Turk alliance with Germany had failed miserably. Brosnahan writes, "With their defeat, the Ottoman Empire collapsed, Istanbul was occupied by the British, and the sultan became a pawn in the hands of the victors."[21]

THE OCCUPATION

The Ottoman Empire had shrunk to the peninsula of Asia Minor and a small piece of the European continent around Istanbul. The Turks really did not control even that. The Entente powers had made secret agreements during the war—if they won, they would divide the Ottoman Empire among themselves. After the truce, Britain occupied Istanbul, Thrace, and the Dardanelles. British, French, and Italian troops entered Anatolia, and Armenia was declared independent.

Sultan Mehmed VI signed the peace treaty, but he could not control the Turkish people, many of whom believed the foreign powers should get out of Turkey. The Turks began fighting for independence from foreign control, the same thing so many of their territories had fought for in the last century. Mustafa Kemal, the hero of Gallipoli, led the new resistance movement.

The rebels forced Istanbul to hold new elections for parliament, and most of the elected wanted national independence. They voted for a National Pact that would give Turkey complete independence, with no legal or financial obligations to the foreign powers. They would give up all claims to former Ottoman territories, except where the majority of people were Turks. The nationalists refused to accept peace on any other terms.

FIGHTING BACK

In response, the Entente powers forced dozens of nationalist leaders out of the country. The rest escaped to Ankara, where they set up a new government. They claimed that while the sultan was a captive of foreigners, the rebel government alone represented the people. Mustafa Kemal was elected president of the Assembly, and for the first time the country was officially called Turkey (*Türkiye*).

Sultan Mehmed VI condemned the rebels to death, though he could not carry out the order from Istanbul. In

1920 he signed the Treaty of Sèvres, which reduced the Ottoman Empire to the northwest corner of Asia Minor. The little that was left to the Ottomans would be run under the close supervision of foreign powers. But the Ankara government refused to accept the treaty.

The rebels began to retake the Anatolian Peninsula. In 1922 Kemal's troops advanced to the British lines in the Dardanelles. The two sides negotiated to avoid a battle. The Treaty of Sèvres was destroyed. At a new peace conference, the Ankara government argued from a position of new power and received most of what they wanted: Istanbul, Thrace, and the Dardanelles.

Turkey also made an unusual arrangement with Greece. The two countries would solve their "minority problems"

Turkish rebels cheer after retaking the Anatolian Peninsula in 1922.

TURKISH CURRENCY

The unit of money in Turkey is called the lira. Because the Turkish economy is weak, Turkish money tends to lose its value compared to strong currencies such as the U.S. dollar and British pound. Over time, a lira is worth less and less, so people need thousands of lira to buy even cheap things. The lowest value coin available today is worth 1,000 lira. The smallest paper note is worth 10,000 lira. Notes go up to 10 million lira. In December 2000, one U.S. dollar was worth 677,621 Turkish liras, up from 81,405 liras in 1996.

Many tourists from Europe, the United States, Australia, and Japan like to visit Turkey because it is inexpensive to stay, eat, and travel there compared to many countries. For example, a loaf of bread costs about 35 cents, and a good restaurant meal may be under five dollars. Although living is cheap in Turkey, many Turks choose to go to other countries where they can make more money. About 1.2 million Turks work abroad, especially in Germany, Saudi Arabia, and France.

A Turkish shopper pays 20,000 lira for several heads of garlic.

through a population exchange, where thousands of people were sent to their ethnic homelands. This solution caused misery among the people affected, about 190,000 Greeks living in western Anatolia and 355,000 Turks living in Greece. Though they were allowed to take money and possessions, they had to leave their homes and businesses. Most moved into poor shantytowns and had trouble finding work. Many of them did not even speak the language of their "home" countries. But the exchange did improve government relations between Greece and Turkey.

THE REPUBLIC

Turkey's new government decided to entirely abolish the power of the sultan. They declared that the national parliament was "the only true representative of the people" and "rests on the principle that the people personally and effectively directs its own destinies."[22] Consequently, Sultan Mehmed VI, the last Ottoman ruler, fled on a British warship.

In October 1923, Ankara became the new capital of the Turkish Republic. The Assembly elected Mustafa Kemal as its first president. Free from foreign interference, the government prepared to face its internal challenges. "The republic," Davison writes, "with its new capital secure in the Anatolian homeland, now set out to make a new Turkey for the Turks, and new Turks for the new Turkey."[23]

Once they had established their power, Kemal's government started reforming the country. Though most Turks were devout Muslims, the new government leaders were less religious and believed Turkey would benefit by imitating secular European countries. The West had power, money, and technology, while most Middle Eastern countries were poor and undeveloped. Turkey adopted the Swiss civil code, the Italian criminal code, and the European calendar in place of the Islamic one. Religion was forced out of all aspects of government.

KEMALISM

In the 1930s, Mustafa Kemal's government described their basic ideals, which they called Kemalism. These six principles were Republicanism, Populism, Statism, Revolutionism, Secularism, and Nationalism. *Republicanism* said that the power to rule belonged to the people, through elected representatives. *Populism* meant the country belonged to everyone, regardless of sex, religion, education, or other differences. The governing body, the Grand National Assembly, was supposed to represent all economic and social interests. With *Statism*, the government tried to improve the economy by investing in industries such as mining, power, agriculture, and railroads. The state, or government, owned many businesses. *Revolutionism* meant continuing change and support for Kemal's reforms.

Secularism meant the separation of religion and government. Kemalists even tried to totally remove religion from public life. Religious shrines were closed. The religious courts were replaced by secular ones. Islamic law had allowed a man to have more than one wife; this practice was now forbidden. Sunday became the official day of rest, as in Europe, instead of Friday, as in the Islamic Middle East.

The last principle, *Nationalism*, intended to build a new national identity to replace the identity lost with the end of the Ottoman Empire. The new focus was on Turkish culture. Minority people, such as the Kurds who made up about 20 percent of the population, were not allowed to express their ethnic identity. Laws kept people from teaching Kurdish or speaking Kurdish in public. This policy set off a Kurdish rebellion in the east. The government executed many of the rebel leaders and moved twenty thousand Kurds away from their homelands to different towns in the west. The early Republican government was determined to achieve their vision at any cost.

MODERNIZATION

The Republican government Westernized many aspects of life besides politics. Arabic script and numbers were replaced by the Latin alphabet and modern Western numbers. Mustafa Kemal hoped that this change would make Turkey more like Europe and also make it easier for people to learn to read. The government even changed the way people dressed. They outlawed the fez, a red felt cap worn by many men, as a sign of the Ottoman past. In an attempt to force people to be less religious, they passed laws prohibiting women from wearing traditional Muslim headscarves in certain public places, such as universities.

Some people fought these new rules, while the politicians attempted to modernize society through strict control. People who resisted the changes were arrested and sometimes executed. The government shut down newspapers and banned other political parties, all in the name of maintaining order. The people's government turned into a regime led by a powerful few, and Kemal ran the country essentially as a dictator. For the Young Turks, historian Erik Zürcher says, "When the choice was between a democratic system with a slower pace of reform and an authoritarian one with more opportunities for radical measures, the second alternative won out."[24] The Young Turks were more concerned with keeping the country strong than with true equality and freedom for all people.

Yet Kemal succeeded in modernizing Turkey at an amazing speed. Zürcher adds, "It is very doubtful whether Turkey would have survived as an independent state without his unique combination of tactical mastery, ruthlessness, realism and sense of purpose. . . . He was absolutely

Pictured is Istanbul in the 1930s. During this time Mustafa Kemal's government modernized Turkey.

Members of Turkey's Democratic Party march at Izmir. The Democratic Party controlled the government from 1950 to 1960.

the right man on the right spot during the greatest crisis in the history of his country and contributed more than anyone else to its survival."[25]

Kemal died in 1938 from cirrhosis of the liver, brought on by years of heavy drinking. He is still Turkey's most important hero, known as Atatürk, "Father of Turkey." His face appears on coins and banknotes, in photos displayed in businesses or private homes, on banners, and even in neon lights. The Popes write, "In many ways, Atatürk has not yet relinquished the hold he had on his nation when he was alive. Frozen in time, his life and achievements have become the stuff of legend. . . . Mustafa Kemal is now a demigod whose every important utterance, and many that are not, must be learnt by heart by schoolchildren."[26]

LEANING TOWARD EUROPE

Kemal's successors continued his policies of modernization and friendship with the West. Turkey tried to remain neutral during World War II, but finally declared war against Germany and Japan in 1945. This time they were on the winning side. After the war, the USSR (Russia) demanded control of the Dardanelles and Turkey's eastern provinces. Turkey turned to the United States for help and received military and financial aid. Turkey joined the United Nations and became a member of NATO, the North Atlantic Treaty Organization. NATO was an agreement between the United States, Canada, and several European countries to defend each other against enemies, particularly the USSR. Turkey's ties to the West were growing.

The people of Turkey demanded more democracy and forced the government to allow opposition parties to form. In 1950, the new Democratic Party won elections and kept control of the government for ten years. This party wanted more private ownership of companies, instead of Kemal's state-owned businesses. Turkey's economy grew quickly, helped by money from the West, especially the United States. Unfortunately, poor management caused economic and social problems. Protests sometimes turned into riots. The government arrested protesters and closed newspapers that reported the problems.

In 1960, the army overthrew the government. The next year they introduced a new constitution that guaranteed freedom of thought, expression, and association, with safeguards to prevent political repression. Open elections were held, but Turkey continued to suffer from weak governments. New political groups sprang up, including a few that used terrorism to promote their views and others that wanted to return to a government based on Islam. No single group had enough power to control the government, however, which suffered from years of weakness and disorganization.

A TROUBLED FRIENDSHIP

In 1974, trouble started over Cyprus, a large island-nation off the southern coast of Turkey. Britain had governed the island as a colony from 1878 until 1960, when Cyprus gained independence. Most of the people were ethnic Greeks, but about one-fifth were Turkish Cypriots. Many Greek Cypriots wanted to reunite with mainland Greece, while the Turkish Cypriots wanted to split the island into two independent countries.

For several years the majority Greeks, backed by soldiers from mainland Greece, put political and military pressure on the Turkish Cypriots. United Nations intervention failed to resolve the issue. In 1974, Turkey invaded the northern part of the island to protect the Turkish Cypriots from attacks by the Greek military and by terrorist groups. The United States suspended military and economic aid to Turkey in protest, so Turkey closed the U.S. military bases in Turkey. In 1978, the United States and Turkey agreed to continue the aid and reopen the bases, but many Turks resented the United States for its interference.

SEARCHING FOR DIRECTION

Turkey's politics continued to grow even more chaotic. A few extreme groups assassinated their opponents, and political demonstrations often turned violent. Some five thousand people were killed between 1978 and 1980. In 1980, with the country on the edge of civil war, the army took over the government again. For two years they banned all political activity, controlled the press, and arrested over one hundred thousand suspected terrorists.

In 1982, the army introduced a new constitution that gave more power to the president and prime minister. In a national vote, 91 percent of the voters approved the constitution, and elections were held the following year. Turgut Özal became prime minister, and later president. During his time in office, the economy improved and violence decreased. Turkey grew closer to the West by supporting the United States in the Gulf War against Iraq in 1990–91.

Özal died of a heart attack in 1993. Though not universally popular, he had given his country direction. After his death, the government once again had too many political parties. Because no group had enough power to govern alone, they had to form coalitions of several political parties. These coalitions often collapsed before any real changes were made. Political scandals linked government leaders to organized crime and terrorism.

Turkey entered the new millennium still struggling with economic and political problems. In 2000, Supreme Court

judge Necdet Sezer became prime minister. He supported democracy and human rights, and many Turks hoped for a better future. Howard states, "A younger generation of Turkish people seemed to join its voices to the chorus of the rest of the world's peoples, calling for a more democratic, more open, more liberal, and more humane public regime."[27]

Turkish Cypriots are imprisoned at a POW camp on Cyprus during the 1974 conflict.

4

DAILY LIFE

Turkey has joined the modern European world in many ways, taking advantage of political, scientific, and economic advances. Yet underneath it all lies a foundation of traditional Muslim religion and culture. These two aspects blend to create a complex and sometimes contradictory way of life for Turkey's 66 million people. Some Turks live much like their ancestors did, but most people have more opportunities. Large cities are more modern and Westernized, while changes take longer to reach the countryside. TV and radio bring Western ideas to more people. Easy travel also exposes people to a wider variety of regional traditions. Though Islam will likely remain the foundation of Turkish life, Western influence will encourage Turkey to keep pace with the fast-changing modern world.

A TURKISH TAKE ON ISLAM

Turkey is officially secular, not governed by religious law. Yet religion influences many aspects of life. About 99 percent of the people in Turkey are Muslims, followers of Islam. The word Islam means "to submit." A Muslim submits to God, who in Arabic is called Allah. This is the same God worshipped by Jews and Christians. In fact, Muslims consider the figures Abraham, Moses, and Jesus to be important prophets. However, they believe that the final and most important prophet is Muhammad, who lived in Arabia from A.D. 570 to 632. Islam requires its followers to pray five times a day and to fast from dawn until dusk during the holy month of Ramadan.

Although most Turks are Muslims, not all Turks follow Islam's strict rules. Many young city dwellers adapt their traditional religion to their modern lifestyles and ignore some of the habits practiced in other Muslim countries. Muslims are not allowed to drink alcohol, and some people believe that

Muslims should not smoke, as Islam forbids unhealthy activities. Yet many Turks drink and smoke. By some estimates, about 60–70 percent of Turkish people in rural areas fast for Ramadan, but only 20–25 percent do so in urban areas. In cities, most businesses and restaurants stay open as usual and Ramadan is celebrated with a street fair. After sunset each night, booths sell food and drink, plus everything from calligraphy passages from the Koran to audio compact discs.

The early leaders of the Republic discouraged religious activity because it was considered old-fashioned and a drawback to economic and social success. Yet Islam has been gaining power again in Turkey. During the 1980s, schools began teaching "religion and ethics." This version of Islam focused on loving one's parents, the government, and the army. More religious content appeared in school books and on government-controlled TV and radio. New mosques were built, more religious schools opened, and many strict Muslims were elected to government office.

Turkish Muslims pray in Ankara. About 99 percent of Turks are Muslims.

A PASSION FOR FOOD

Turkish food is considered some of the best in the world. Most Turkish food is healthy, as the diet is based on grains, vegetables, and fruits, with meat and dairy products used sparingly. Even the most common form of fat, olive oil, has health benefits. Common ingredients include fish, rice, beans, eggplants, zucchini, tomatoes, bell peppers, and garlic. Yogurt is eaten plain but also used in sauces, soups, and salads.

For breakfast, people usually eat bread and jam, white goat cheese, black olives, and tea. Children may carry a handful of mixed nuts and raisins in the pockets of their school uniform as a healthy snack before exams. Many workplaces provide lunch, while other workers purchase something from a street stand. "Fast food" usually means roast lamb or mutton, sliced thin, and laid on a roll. In the afternoon, women often get together for tea, where the host serves a fancy assortment of pastries and cakes.

Dinner starts with soup. The meat and vegetable main course follows, along with a salad. The next course contains vegetables marinated in olive oil, followed by dessert and fruit. The most common sweets are small pastries soaked in honey and rosewater. They often contain sesame seeds or pistachio nuts. Puddings or custards may also be served as desserts. *Lokum*, known elsewhere as Turkish Delight, is a soft jelly candy sometimes flavored with fruit or nuts. Coffee, made very strong and served in tiny cups, is usually drunk after the meal. At a party where drinks are served, the guests start with appetizers, often spread out on a table set up in the garden or on the balcony. Dinner is served much later.

Food is especially important during holidays and family outings. In nice weather, families may travel into the countryside for an elaborate picnic. They plan who will make the various dishes—rice pilafs, stuffed grape leaves, meatballs, salads, fruit, and drinks. Then they load rugs, hammocks, pillows, copper charcoal burners, samovars (urns for making tea), and musical instruments into the car, and head off on an excursion known as "stealing a day from fate."

The battle between modern secular ideas and strict Islamic rules causes some conflict in Turkey. In general, religious devotion is seen as a matter of personal choice, but questions of alcohol use, modesty of dress for women, relations between men and women, and public displays of affection can cause tension between traditional Muslims and less religious people.

CHILDHOOD

No matter how devout a Turk is, chances are that Islam influences the ceremonies of birth and childhood, which are still honored with traditional practices. People are having fewer children today, but children are still highly valued. In fact, Turkey was the first country to declare a national holiday honoring children. April 23 is Children's Day, now an international holiday recognized by the United Nations. May 19, Mustafa Kemal's birthday, is also celebrated in Turkey as National Youth and Sports Day.

When a new bride gets pregnant with her first child, her family is particularly excited. In the countryside a woman declares her pregnancy by wearing clothing or scarves marked with special symbols. Midwives help women give birth in rural areas, but in cities most women now give birth in hospitals. A new mother gets presents of gold and her child gets all kinds of gifts from relatives, friends, and neighbors. After giving birth, the mother is supposed to stay home for forty days, so if she has a job, she gets a long break. The child is named during a special ceremony during which a religious leader or a family elder holds the child facing Mecca. He reads from the Koran into the child's left ear and repeats the child's new name three times into the right ear.

When they are nine or ten years old, Muslim boys in Turkey have a special ceremony for their circumcision, the surgical removal of the foreskin on the penis. Circumcision is a symbol of the boy's admission into Islam, similar to confirmation for Catholics and the bar mitzvah for Jews. Muslim boys dress in a white suit with a hat, cape, and red satin sash. "On the day of the operation," Brosnahan writes, "the boy is dressed in the special suit, visits relatives and friends, and leads a parade—formerly on horseback, now in cars—around his neighbourhood or city, attended by musicians and merrymakers." In the afternoon, the quick circumcision operation is performed at a clinic or hospital. A celebration follows, with music and food. "The newly circumcised lad attends, resting in bed, as his friends and relatives bring him gifts and congratulate him on having entered manhood."[28]

A few people today ignore tradition and have the circumcision performed just after a boy's birth, before he goes home from the hospital. Families with several boys may have all their sons circumcised at the same time, so the children may be anywhere from two to fourteen years old. In rural areas, whole villages sometimes join together to share the expense of a circumcision feast. Wealthy families sometimes include poor boys or orphans in their sons' ceremonies. For boys, circumcision is an important step in growing up.

A FOCUS ON LEARNING

Though the circumcision ceremony has not changed much over the centuries, daily life has for children. During the Ottoman Empire, few boys went to school, and almost no girls did. Most people did not know how to read. The Turkish Republic changed that. Education is now required by law for both boys and girls from ages seven to fourteen. Children study math, natural sciences, the Turkish language, history, geography, music, and art. They also learn patriotism and civic responsibility.

The Republican government wanted to educate all young Turks so they would be prepared to enter the modern world as skilled workers. Unfortunately, the government has a hard time enforcing compulsory education. The population of Turkey has grown so quickly that half the people today are younger than age twenty. The educational system cannot keep up with the growing number of children. Schools have trouble getting enough classroom space, supplies, and teachers. In cities, schools may have fifty students in one class, whereas in the countryside, students may have to walk to another village to attend school. Many children, especially in small villages or the countryside, quit school to work on farms or in factories.

Primary school students wear black uniforms with white collars, and many secondary schools also have uniforms. Students pay to attend secondary school and must compete to get into the best ones, because space is limited. Some students go to private schools run by American, English, French, or German organizations, where many of the classes are taught in the foreign language. Other students attend technical training schools that focus on subjects such as secretarial skills, tourism, or various trades. Since the 1990s, more young people have been attending religious schools. About 10 percent of high-school students go to Muslim teacher-training schools.

YOUTH ACTIVITIES

Most Turkish children and teens live much like Western young people. School takes up most of their time, and they

often have two to three hours of homework a night. In their free time, they may watch TV, go to movies, or play video games. In rural areas, which may only have one or two televisions per village and no movie theaters, kids spend more time playing traditional games such as tag and jump rope.

Boys and girls in Turkey between the ages of seven and fourteen are required to attend school.

Sports are popular for both spectators and players. Soccer is the favorite sport, but people also enjoy basketball, wrestling, archery, weight lifting, tennis, karate, swimming, and many others. Some athletic events are little known in the rest of the world. A pastime called *cirit* reflects the Turk's long-standing love of horses, according to journalist Stephen Kinzer. "Cirit matches are lightning-fast, played by riders who gallop toward each other in clouds of dust, hurling wooden javelins. They win points by striking an opponent or forcing his horse to veer off course."[29] Oil wrestling is another sport popular with men and boys. Wrestlers fight shirtless, in leather trousers, drenched head to foot in olive oil.

All men in Turkey, like this member of the special forces, must serve in the military.

Turkey's general directorate of youth and sports provides sports facilities and youth centers throughout the country. They promote scouting activities, youth camps and festivals, chess tournaments, and training in folk music and dance. Children also spend a lot of time with their families. On summer evenings families may stroll the streets chatting with neighbors. On Sundays, they might go to a town park for a picnic. Children also get involved in politics early. Because there are so many of them, young people can influence the government, especially after they are allowed to vote at age eighteen.

A YOUNG MAN'S SERVICE

Teens can choose to go to military high schools or military war academies starting at age fifteen. They are not considered members of the armed forces, however, until they begin their official service. The constitution states that national service is the duty of every Turk, so all Turkish men must enter the army. Anyone who refuses is jailed, even if they claim a moral disapproval of warfare. There is no conscientious objector status and no alternative service, although some people would like to change that. Normal military service is eighteen months long, and training starts at age nineteen. University students can put off serving until the age of twenty-eight, and can then serve shorter terms as officers. Turkey's military of about six hundred thousand soldiers includes over four hundred thousand draftees serving their required time. Women may serve in the military and are especially recruited as officers, but since women are not required to serve, most soldiers are men.

According to the Turkish Embassy in Washington, D.C., "The activities of the military are not confined to the defense of the country only but are also oriented towards creating new values and making social, economic and educational contributions to society as a whole."[30] The education and training young men receive in the Turkish Armed Forces is supposed to help unite boys from different backgrounds. In

TURKISH DRESS

During the days of the Ottoman empire, Ottoman men wore a loose, ankle-length robe called a caftan, over baggy trousers, a shirt, and a jacket with a wide sash. They wore soft leather socks, and leather slippers or heavier leather overshoes. All Muslim women, like the Byzantine Christians before them, wore veils when outside their homes.

Rules determined the color and cut of the clothes men could wear, so everyone would know their rank. The sultan's advisors wore green, his chamberlains scarlet, and religious officials purple. Greeks wore pale blue skullcaps and black shoes. Jews wore yellow caps and blue shoes. Armenians wore dark blue caps and violet shoes. Only Muslim men could wear turbans, a long piece of cloth wrapped around the head. Even these were regulated, so no man could wear a turban taller than the sultan's.

Those men who could afford it wore rich decorations just as the women did. Noel Barber writes in *The Sultans*, "This was the age of flashing jewels on turban and scimitar, of ostrich plumes, of flowing robes, of immense pantaloons or drawers, of sable-lined pelisses, but each man knew his neighbour instantly by the clothes which strict law demanded he must wear." Children dressed in styles similar to their parents.

In 1826 Sultan Mahmud II changed court dress. Most men began wearing European style pants and jackets, with a red cap called a fez, which was banned in 1925. After the founding of the Republic, some women began adopting European clothing as well. Today many Turks wear Western-style clothing, but some, especially in rural areas, still wear baggy pants, long robes, and headscarves or turbans.

Men wear traditional Turkish dress.

addition to technical training, they should gain a social conscience and respect for Turkish history and culture.

Many Turks consider military service to be an important part of life. Men are not considered successful until they perform their military service among other things. Before starting, boys get a two-month vacation to enjoy themselves. In the last week they visit friends and relatives to say goodbye and receive presents. Boys are sent off to the military with music, prayers, and advice. Any letters sent home during their service are treasured and shared. When a young man has served his time, his family may cook a special sweet and offer it to neighbors, relatives, and friends, who come to congratulate the family. The young man can now begin his life as an adult. He can take a job or return to school, but he will not be considered a complete success until he marries and starts a family.

A couple marries in a traditional ceremony. Marriage and dating practices differ in rural and urban Turkey.

MARRIAGE

In the past, marriages often were arranged by the couple's parents, sometimes even when the children were babies. The husband's family paid the bride's parents money, and she usually went to live with her husband's family after marriage. The Republican government made arranged marriages illegal, as part of their attempt to increase the rights of women. Yet in rural areas a young man who wants to marry may still send his female relatives to look for a bride for him. Most couples do not get to know each other very well before marrying, and are never left alone together. In fact, many country girls are married young to men they have never seen. They then "belong" to their husbands. In cities, more couples today meet directly, perhaps through their jobs or schools.

The families of the bride and groom first have a formal meeting where they agree to the marriage. Later, they have an engagement party. Guests gather at the groom's home and then go to the bride's home for lunch. The groom's female relatives dress the bride in a special dress, and she is given jewelry. The groom's family pays for the wedding, which may last several days. On the first day a wedding flag is planted at the groom's home. That night, the bride's hands are painted with a natural dye called henna, while she spends time with all her female friends and relatives.

In the past, elderly women helped prepare the bride for her wedding, but today it is more often a professional hairdresser. The bride wears a cherry-red dress and a long veil. Traditionally, the men and women are kept separate. The religious leader will ask the bride and groom whether they agree to marry. Then he reads from the Koran. The groom goes to the women's area where he gives gifts to the bride's sisters and receives the blessings of the elder women. Afterward, the women and men eat dinner separately. Following the meal, the groom and bride are seated together with a long scarf covering their heads. They read prayers and are allowed to see each other only reflected in mirrors.

That night the groom sleeps in the bride's house, but in a separate room. The next afternoon the bride says goodbye to her family, then the wedding procession travels around the neighborhood and finally to the groom's house. These traditions vary by region, and in some cases are ignored altogether today.

The legal minimum age for marriage is eighteen. Girls often marry by age twenty, boys when they are a few years older. Young people in cities tend to marry later than those in the countryside. In order to be legal, marriages have to be conducted by a government agent rather than a religious leader. About half of Turkish people have both legal and religious ceremonies. About 40 percent of weddings do not have a religious ceremony, while 10 percent are only religious and therefore not recognized by law. However the union is celebrated, marriage is a turning point in a person's life.

A WOMAN'S PLACE

Women are especially affected by marriage, as tradition pressures them to dedicate their lives to serving their husbands and children. Change is slowest in rural areas and small villages. There the father still rules the family, and women may live much like their great-grandmothers did. Women are considered little more than property, and have few rights. They are expected to obey their father, their husband, and even their adult sons. They usually follow a traditional modest dress code and cover their hair. Virginity is so important that a girl who has sex before marriage may be murdered by her family.

Still, many Turkish women have more freedom than women in most Middle Eastern countries. Since the 1920s, they have been legally equal to men. By law, women have the same educational opportunities and career choices, allowing them to earn their own livings and be less dependent on men. They are no longer required to get their husbands' permission to hold a job or travel abroad, and must get equal pay for equal work. They also have equal rights in divorce, child custody, and inheritance.

But although women are officially equal to men, they may have a hard time claiming their rights. For example, even though women can legally divorce, in rural areas it is not acceptable for a woman to live alone, and her family may not take her back. "Ataturk gave Turkish women equal status, in theory at least," the Popes write, "but society took a long time to digest the change. . . . Schoolbooks still reinforce the attitude that 'the father is the head of the family, and the wife, who does the cooking and looks after the children, is his assistant and companion.'"[31]

President Bill Clinton meets with Turkey's first female prime minister, Tansu Ciller, in 1995.

In their struggle to become truly equal, women have formed organizations to lobby for women's rights; they have started a home for battered women in Istanbul; and most importantly, they pursue education and work in many fields. Over 9 million of the 23 million working people in Turkey are women. Today Turkish women are journalists, bank clerks and managers, teachers, business leaders, police and army officers, engineers, executives, artists, and politicians. The percentage of women stockbrokers and lawyers is higher than in many European countries. Nearly two-thirds of health workers, including doctors and pharmacists, are women. Few women hold high elected positions, but some arc senior government officials and judges. In 1993, Tansu Ciller was elected Turkey's first female prime minister, with much of her support coming unexpectedly from conservative eastern Anatolia.

DEATH

Burial rituals in Turkey today are much like they have been
for centuries. In traditional Islamic practice, when someone
dies, the body is laid on a bed with the person's head facing
Mecca and the eyelids closed. A muezzin, a Muslim crier
who calls the hour of daily prayer, announces the funeral
time and place from the mosque, and recites passages from
the Koran.

The burial should take place as soon as possible during
daylight, either the day of death or the next day. First the body
is washed in a special way. A woman must be washed by a
woman, and a man by a man. Then the body is dressed in a
white shroud and put in a wooden coffin, which is covered
with a piece of green cloth and carried to the courtyard of a
mosque. People in the street stand silently and salute the funeral procession. Mourners pray inside the mosque, then join
the religious leader in the courtyard for the funeral service.

A hearse carries the coffin to the cemetery while mourners follow in other cars. They are silent, and should not cry.
The deceased is removed from the coffin and buried only in
the shroud, with the body lying on its right side facing
Mecca. The religious leader prays at the burial, and the deceased is also remembered with prayers on the seventh and
fifty-second days after death.

Life expectancy in Turkey is about seventy-one years
(slightly less for men and more for women), almost ten
years below the European average. This is in part because
of infant mortality rates of almost 5 percent, which are better than the world average of 6 to 7 percent, but worse than
the European average of less than 2 percent. Medical advances are helping people to live longer, but people need
better access to health care, especially in the poorer eastern
provinces. However long people live, their deaths are
mourned in traditional ways. Like other important aspects
of life, this final passage is influenced by traditional Islamic
beliefs.

ARTS AND ENTERTAINMENT

"A heart in love with beauty never grows old," says a Turkish proverb. The love of beauty in the form of art goes back thousands of years in Turkey. The Romans created intricate mosaic murals, the Byzantines ornately decorated their churches, and the Ottomans covered mosques and palaces with painted tiles. Today the arts in Turkey combine these ancient influences with modern experimentation.

ISLAMIC ART

The first followers of Islam had few artistic traditions of their own. As they conquered other empires, they combined the art forms they found. Roman, Byzantine, Persian, and Central Asian styles all influenced Islamic art. Islam, however, prohibits art showing humans or animals. This was meant to prevent people from worshipping images of prophets or saints; only God should be worshipped. Also, artists were not supposed to create images of living creatures, because only God is able to create life. "This prohibition determined the course of Islamic art," writes Brosnahan. "It would be rich in architecture, calligraphy, stained glass, manuscript illumination, glass-blowing, marquetry, metalwork and other geometric design, but would have little painting or sculpture as those arts are understood in non-Islamic countries."[32]

Upper-class Ottomans sometimes showed interest in European artistic styles, but the average Turk only saw traditional Islamic art forms. That changed in 1923, with the founding of the secular Turkish Republic. Brosnahan continues, "All at once . . . artists of both genders were encouraged to create paintings, sculptures, plays, films and musical scores portraying the entire range of human activity and emotion."[33] The government supported new art schools, museums, opera and dance companies, and orchestras.

Hundreds of "People's Houses" all over Turkey introduced villagers to a variety of artistic and cultural activities. The modern Turkish Republic encourages artists to explore new forms, but artists of all types still often draw on traditional subjects and techniques.

ARCHITECTURE

Turkey is famous for its architecture. The great cultures that controlled Asia Minor all showed off their power with impressive buildings. Two of the seven works of art and architecture considered by the ancient Greeks and Romans to be the Seven Wonders of the World are in Turkey: the Temple of Artemis at Ephesus and the Mausoleum of Halicarnassus, though only fragments of both remain. Other ancient structures still dot the country, from the ruins of Roman temples to Christian churches cut into the rock cliffs of Cappadocia.

The most well-preserved architecture is more recent, from the Ottoman reign. Many famous buildings were designed by

It took more than 3,500 workers seven years to complete the Suleiman Mosque.

one man, Mimar Sinan, who lived from about 1491 to 1588. Sinan worked as an engineer for the Ottoman army until he was in his forties, when Sultan Suleiman hired him as court architect. Sinan supervised the building of over three hundred structures throughout the Empire, including mosques, religious schools, hospitals, baths, caravansaries, kitchens, bridges, and aqueducts. Sinan used a Byzantine-style dome in many mosques, including Suleiman's Mosque, considered the finest Ottoman building in Istanbul. Over thirty-five hundred laborers worked on this mosque for seven years. A huge dome with high windows lets in light. In the evening, hundreds of lamps glow from metal rings hung from the ceiling. Stonecutters, wood-carvers, metalworkers, glassworkers, and ceramic artists made the carved doors, stained-glass windows, and tiles for the interior. The mosque complex also contains a religious school, a soup kitchen, baths, and the tombs of Suleiman and Roxelana. Novelist Mary Lee Settle described her impressions of Sinan's work: "He created gentle spaces, sheltering without diminishing, soaring without losing a sense of the human, and alive with color, always color, refined and glowing, and filled with quietness."[34]

In the late eighteenth and nineteenth centuries, architects began copying European styles. Many buildings from that time are so ornate they seem garish today. Dolmabahce Palace, along the shore of the Bosporus, has about 285 rooms and 43 large halls. The Ceremonial Hall holds the largest chandelier in the world, with 750 crystals, a present from Queen Victoria of England. The rooms were decorated and stuffed full of European furniture, carpets, paintings, and art objects. The last home of the sultans, Dolmabahce Palace today is a museum.

Modern buildings are often suburban homes or high-rise apartments and offices similar to those found around the world. Still, Turks grow up surrounded by historic architectural wonders. They may go to school in a building converted from a medieval covered market. Neighborhood mosques are built to classic standards. Some public baths are still open for business after hundreds of years. Many architects today draw on classic designs but use modern construction techniques to create buildings that suit current standards of comfort. Turks have won international awards for restoring old structures using the standards of historic preservation.

For example, one sixteenth century caravansary has been restored as a modern hotel.

DECORATIVE ARTS

Turkish public buildings are often filled with ornate decorations. Because Islamic art cannot depict people or animals, Turkish art has traditionally featured geometric designs, leaf shapes, and script. Geometric and floral designs have great symbolism in Islamic art. The repeating patterns represent the divine energy that radiates through the universe. The natural grace of Arabic writing encouraged the use of calligraphy as decoration. Because the Koran is so important in Islam and Koranic verses are meant to encourage spiritual thought, passages from that holy book often decorate religious buildings such as mosques.

Many calligraphy styles developed over the centuries. A strong, blocky form was popular for use on buildings and stonework. One elegant script is used most often in copies of the Koran. More delicate forms were used for literature or for writing people's titles. The sultan's monogram, used to sign official documents, became a work of art, often decorated with gold leaf. Some calligraphers wrote texts into the shapes of stars, flowers, or mosques. According to Horst-Meijer, "The final aim of calligraphers was not legibility, for the Koran was known by heart. The more difficult a text was to read and the more skillfully it was executed, the more esteem was gained."[35]

Islam also discouraged the use of precious materials such as gold, silver, and gems. Instead, Islamic art focused on ceramics, wood carving, and bronze. Pottery was such an important art form that vessels became works of beauty instead of just practical containers. Chinese porcelain influenced Islamic pottery, though potters had to adapt their techniques to the local clay. They also adapted Chinese styles to local tastes. Ottoman artists made pots with Chinese blue and white designs, but also with Turkish floral patterns in green, turquoise, purple, brown, and black.

Flat tiles were used to decorate buildings. Glazed brick and colorful ceramic tile often covered the insides of mosques, palaces, and baths from floor to ceiling. Colored tile production reached its high point during the sixteenth

1,001 ARABIAN NIGHTS

The *Arabian Nights* is a collection of Persian, Arabian, Egyptian, and Indian folktales handed down over the centuries. The earliest known version of *The Arabian Nights* is a ninth-century papyrus text in which one character asks another, a woman named Scheherazade, to tell a story. Additional stories were added over the years; some of the best known tales, including *Sindbad the Sailor* and *Aladdin*, may be late additions. In many of the early texts, stories that are obviously fiction are claimed by the authors to be fact. Perhaps some storytellers drew on real incidents for inspiration, or maybe these were early versions of "urban legends" that got more exciting as they were passed along by word of mouth.

Eventually the stories settled into a standard format, written down in its present form by the late 1400s. The stories begin when the sultan discovers that his wife has been unfaithful. He has her killed, and to prevent any future wife from being unfaithful, he vows to marry a different woman every night and have her killed at dawn. Scheherazade marries the sultan, but that night she begins telling a story to her sister. She stops in the middle of the story, and the sultan allows her to live another day so he can hear the ending. This continues for 1001 nights, until the sultan realizes he loves Scheherazade too much to kill her.

Europeans first met *The Thousand and One Nights* in 1704. Antoine Galland, an assistant to the French ambassador, purchased a Syrian copy of the manuscript in Istanbul. He translated it into French and published a dozen volumes. The original manuscript probably never had 1,001 stories; that number may simply have been used to mean "a lot." But Europeans wanted the whole 1,001 nights, so translators added other Arabic stories. Although many of the stories are a thousand years old, later translators adapted them to the fifteenth-century setting of the Ottoman Empire, with its beauty and luxury. The originals were clearly written for adults. Sex, alcohol, and drug use are common themes. But because the stories contain many fantasy elements—magical spells and genies granting wishes—in the West the stories were rewritten as children's literature. Besides remaining popular entertainment, *The Arabian Nights* have given scholars a unique glimpse of past Middle Eastern culture.

and seventeenth centuries, but modern tile makers continue the tradition. Decorative tiles, bowls, and platters are popular tourist items sold in local bazaars. Most are decorated with traditional floral, geometric, or calligraphy designs, but some now ignore Islamic rules and include representational images such as fish, animals, or famous people like Atatürk.

A woman rests near a Turkish carpet shop. The country is famous for its bright, intricately woven carpets.

CARPETS

Turkish women have been weaving carpets for over two thousand years, using many of the same designs as other decorative arts. For nomadic tribes, carpets were furniture, adding warmth and color to a tent-home. They were used as hanging screens, wall tapestries, cushions, and prayer rugs as well as floor coverings. Village women wove carpets for their families. They memorized traditional patterns, but also personalized their work by choosing a pattern and colors that suited their own taste. Women worked hard on these carpets, according to Brosnahan. "Knowing they would be judged on their efforts, the women took great care over their handiwork, hand-spinning and dyeing the wool, and choosing what they judged to be the most interesting and beautiful patterns."[36]

Each region has its own traditional weaving methods and designs. Some patterns were handed down through the generations, and a few date back even to prehistoric times, although people also develop new designs. Geometric shapes and floral patters are popular, but today weavers also use birds, animals, and dragons. Prayer carpets have the shape of a mosque prayer niche in the middle, while other carpets show a village with houses and mosques, or stylized nomadic tent camps. Carpet designs sometimes use symbols that can be read only by knowledgeable people. Stylized eagles are a symbol of freedom, while the scorpion represents pride.

Even the dye colors vary by region, depending on what materials are available. Carpets from eastern Anatolia are often dark brown because the sheep in that area have dark wool. Wool or silk for carpets was traditionally colored with vegetable dyes made from flowers, leaves, roots, or fruits. Some common colors come from onion skins, walnuts, and tobacco. Today chemical dyes are sometimes used.

In the nineteenth century, Europeans started buying Turkish carpets. Men ran companies to sell carpets made by local women. Turkey is still famous for its carpets, and many shops sell them to tourists. In small villages, a man may buy looms and yarn and set up a small business with his wife and daughters. Girls aged ten to twenty are often considered the best weavers, because their sharp eyes and small fingers can handle the delicate work of making over six hundred double knots in one square inch.

Many weavers ignore local traditions and make whatever they think will sell. Sometimes they create one-of-a-kind patterns, or even copy photographs. In other cases, women weave a standard design requested by the store, without any individual creativity. The work may even be divided among several people. Turkey's Ministry of Culture is trying to preserve traditional carpet-making techniques by sponsoring projects that use the old ways of dyeing and weaving. An average, medium-size carpet takes from six to twelve weeks to weave by hand. The best silk carpets take up to a year of work.

VISUAL ARTS

Islamic artists often made everyday objects such as carpets into works of beauty, but they seldom made individual works of art that had no purpose except to be beautiful. Traditionally, art was meant to decorate useful objects, not to stand on its own. Islamic painters did not paint canvasses to hang on the wall; instead painting was usually applied to book illustration. Texts of history, science, and poetry were decorated in bright colors, including silver and gold. Sometimes Ottoman illustrators broke the rule against representational figures and showed life scenes from the royal court and the military. Miniature paintings were also popular with European visitors to Turkey in the time before photography. Travelers who wanted a pictorial record of their trip could hire bazaar painters who would make quick sketches of street scenes.

In the late nineteenth century, upper-class Ottomans started showing interest in European-style painting. Some even had their portraits painted. An Academy of Fine Arts was opened in Istanbul in 1883. Initially most of the teachers were foreign and many of the students were Greek or Armenian, with only a few Turks. The school taught painting, sculpture, architecture, and engraving. The Ottoman Painter's Society was formed in 1909 and staged exhibitions from 1916 until 1952. The School of Fine Arts for Women opened in 1914. During the Republic, painting grew in popularity. Turkish painting started to focus more on figures, including nudes, which had been common subjects in Europe for centuries. As more young artists traveled to Europe, they brought back modern art styles such as cubism and expressionism. In the 1940s some artists started adding regional folk art elements to their works. In the 1960s, artists explored social issues with realistic paintings.

The Academy of Fine Arts still influences modern art as Turkish painters explore new forms. Artists today can find a home for their work in museums, galleries, and private collections. Nearly five hundred museums in Turkey display art, archeological remains, or both.

LITERATURE

Like visual arts, literature during the Ottoman Empire was influenced heavily by Islam. Science and history were presented from a religious viewpoint. Fictional novels were uncommon and poetry focused on Islam. According to Brosnahan, "Ottoman poets, borrowing from the great Arabic and Persian traditions, wrote sensual love poems of attraction, longing, fulfilment and ecstasy in the search for union with God."[37] Poetry was often sung to the accompaniment of musical instruments, either in rich Ottoman households or publicly by wandering performers.

In the late 1800s, European literature started influencing Ottoman writers. After the founding of the Republic, writers

A painting in a coffeehouse shows the artist's attention to Turkish dress and customs.

began using everyday language instead of the formalized and long-winded style of the Ottoman court. Nationwide literacy increased when the new government focused on education and introduced a Turkish alphabet based on Latin letters to replace Arabic script.

Writers began exploring political issues and writing about the hard lives of rural peasants. They wrote realistic novels, poems, and plays that explored patriotism, social justice, and everyday life in their country. A few writers have been translated into other languages for readers outside of Turkey. Orhan Pamuk writes novels, either historical or set in the present day, that explore philosophical ideas. He is Turkey's best-selling author and his work is read and admired in other countries as well. Yashar Kemal (no relation to Mustafa), the author of dozens of books, has been nominated several times for the Nobel Prize for Literature. His 1961 book *Mehmed, My Hawk*, features a Turkish Robin Hood who helps the poor and fights injustice. Kemal also received an award for his

HOCA: MUSLIM PHILOSOPHER

Turks enjoy folktales, including some that are centuries old and last for up to thirty hours. Nasrettin Hoca is the hero of many popular stories. Hoca, a thirteenth-century teacher, was famous for the funny anecdotes he used to make important philosophical points. Stories such as this one are popular among Turks:

> Once the Hoca was resting in the shade of a walnut tree on a hot day. He gazed out over a nearby field of watermelons. "I do not understand the ways of Allah," the Hoca thought. "Tiny walnuts grow on a strong tree, and huge watermelons grow on a thin vine. If I were the Creator, I would put the watermelons on the tree, and the walnuts on the vines."

> Just then, a walnut fell on the Hoca's head. He looked up and rubbed the sore spot. "Forgive me, Allah," he said. "Your wisdom is greater than mine. I am glad that watermelons don't grow on trees."

> In another story, the Hoca declares that horses would be more useful if they could fly. Then a pigeon flies over him and releases droppings on his head. Once again, the Hoca realizes the wisdom of Allah, who kept horses from flying.

dedication to human rights and freedom of expression. He was arrested in 1996 for "inciting racial hatred" after he wrote articles criticizing the Turkish government for its oppression of Turkey's Kurdish minority. Though the government officially promotes literature, officials have punished authors who criticize the government. Many Turkish writers have been imprisoned for writing about social problems or have had their work banned. Turkish authors are trying hard to express their political and artistic visions, despite government interference.

MUSIC

Politicians censor music just as they do many other areas of Turkish life. Authorities have banned some artists and even whole styles of music thought to be immoral or antigovernment. In the early years of the Republic, the only government-approved styles of music were Western classical and traditional Turkish folk music. In the 1990s, independent radio and TV stations broke the government's hold on music. Now listeners in Turkey can hear all kinds of music, from ancient to modern. Chamber music groups and symphony orchestras perform European classics. In the summer, the International Istanbul Music Festival showcases local and foreign performances of modern and classical music, opera, ballet, and theater. One favorite is an opera by Wolfgang Amadeus Mozart, *Abduction from the Seraglio*, which is performed in Topkapi Palace where the opera is set.

For a thousand years, Turkish wandering musician-poets sang songs of love, death, heroes, and legends. Today they have been replaced largely by radio and recorded music. Yet some of their songs, dating as far back as the sixteenth century, remain popular. The most common traditional instruments are drums, wooden flutes, and stringed instruments such as the lute. Traditional Turkish musical styles, such as Ottoman classical, religious, and some folk music, may sound strange to foreigners. Instead of the Western system of octaves with whole and half tones, Turkish music uses a system

A Turkish man plays his drum at a music festival. Common instruments in Turkish music are drums, wooden flutes, and stringed instruments.

A traveling group of whirling dervishes performs in London. They believe their symbolic dances bring them closer to God.

of modalities that also includes quarter tones. To the untrained ear, quarter tones can sound flat.

Throughout the twentieth century, Turkish music drew heavily on European and American styles. Many Western groups are popular in Turkey, but today local artists have taken center stage. Sanaat uses eighteenth century vocal styles. Turku blends a mix of Turkish, Arabic, and Western instruments. Modern rock musicians often draw on traditional musical styles and instruments, for a blend that is purely Turkish.

DANCE

By some estimates Turkey has nearly ten thousand native folk songs and dances. In rural areas, every event has a special song and dance—from births, weddings, festivals, and deaths to sowing the fields or harvesting the crops. Some songs express romantic love, longing for home, a wish for fertility, or the desire for good luck. Each region has its own folk dance, which may have been performed in the same way for hundreds of years. People wear special costumes for these dances, each handmade works of art. Even their socks are woven with patterns that have hidden meanings. The government sponsors dance classes for young people so these folk dances will not be forgotten.

The whirling dervishes perform a type of dance quite different from what Westerners know. Dervishes were Muslim monks, and this particular order was founded in the thirteenth century. Whirling dervishes believe they can know Allah better through ritual dance. They spin in circles for many minutes until they enter a trance, intended to help them open themselves to God's love. Dervishes were banned after the founding of the Republic, but in recent years they have been allowed to perform again. They wear long, white robes symbolizing the death shroud and red cone-shaped hats symbolizing tombstones. As they spin to music played on flutes, violins, and drums, they attempt to channel the energy that makes the world turn. They cast off black cloaks representing tombs, ritually leaving the tomb of the self and setting aside worldly ties.

Another ancient form of dance popular today is Oryantal, known in the West as Oriental Dance or belly dancing. In the

 ## A CONTROVERSIAL POET

Nazim Hikmet (1902–1963) is considered Turkey's greatest poet of the twentieth century, but he was jailed for over eighteen years, and finally exiled from Turkey, for writing about controversial issues. He wrote some of his best work in jail, such as *Istanbul House of Detention*, which included this passage:

My love, they're on the march: heads forward, eyes wide open, the red glare of burning cities, crops trampled, endless footsteps.

And people slaughtered: like trees and calves only easier and faster.

My love, amid these footsteps and this slaughter I sometimes lost my freedom, bread, and you, but never my faith in the days that will come out of the darkness, screams, and hunger to knock on our door with hands full of sun.

Midde East, belly dancing is seen as an expression of feminine grace and creativity. Over the centuries, women performed Oryantal dance for each other during celebrations or informal get-togethers. The undulating belly movements strengthened the pelvic muscles to make giving birth easier. When a woman went into labor, her female relatives would perform the dance to symbolically help the birth. Today professional dancers sometimes perform for tourists in restaurants or clubs, while other women still dance for fun with their friends.

THEATER

Because Islamic women traditionally did not take part in public life, the Ottoman Empire did not see many public dance or theater performances. Dance was primarily a private activity, performed among family members. Under the Turkish Republic, public performances by men and women are encouraged, so in the last century, dance and theater have developed in Turkey. The State Opera and Ballet Company gives performances throughout the country.

Theater suffers from competition with TV and videos, but still has a presence, especially in Istanbul. Groups perform traditional and modern dramas and comedies, including works by famous Europeans such as William Shakespeare. Though live theater was seldom performed during the Ottoman Empire, shadow-puppet theater was popular. The puppets are made from see-through animal skins painted in bright colors. A light projects the puppet images onto a white screen between them and the audience.

Most shadow-puppet shows were comical. The two main characters, Karagoz and his sidekick Hazivad, were always arguing. Their wit made them fun to watch and hid the political satire that often criticized the sultan. Stories were ongoing, like a soap opera, and explored everyday life instead of the traditional religious themes. Shadow-puppet theater is dying out, as few people today want to spend the long hours needed to make the puppets and learn to handle them. The government is trying to preserve this part of its Ottoman heritage with an annual Shadow Play and Traditional Turkish Theater Contest. Turkish artists may explore new art forms, but Turkey does not want to lose its cultural traditions.

TODAY'S CHALLENGES

Turkey has cultural and religious ties to the Arab world, but struggles to grow economically and politically closer to Europe. One important goal is admission into the European Union (EU), a group of nations that work together for their political and economic benefit. Using the EU's form of money, the euro, would help Turkey's economy because the euro is much more stable than Turkey's own currency, the lira. The EU would also provide Turkey with a large market to sell their goods, and Turks could work in other EU countries without restriction.

Turkey is a candidate for the EU, but has been waiting since 1987 for acceptance. If Turkey enters the European Union, it will take a place of power in Europe. Turkey has a larger landmass than any EU country, and within a few decades, will probably have the largest population. As part of the EU, Turkey would be in a position to also influence world events. However, the country must make advances in its political system and economy before it can be admitted.

The necessary changes have been slow in coming, in large part because not all Turks agree on the path their country should take to the future. Some people would like to see Turkey turn away from Europe and draw closer to the Islamic world. According to Kinzer, the question for Turkey is, "Should it look east or west, turn toward its Asian or its European heritage, take the risks of democracy or remain wrapped in comfortable paternalism?"[38]

ISLAM AND POLITICS

Turkey officially has a secular, Western-style democratic government. Religion is separate from government and the power rests with the people, who vote for elected representatives. Some Turkish politicians want an Islamic political

Supporters of the pro-Islamic Welfare Party celebrate their group's success in Turkey's 1995 national election.

system instead, where all laws would be based on the Koran. The government's policies often have promoted educated city people to succeed, while villagers remain stuck in poverty. Islam, with its focus on charity and honesty, became the voice of the poor in politics. But most of the politicians in power hold Mustafa Kemal's ideal of a secular government and are afraid of Islam's influence in politics. From the start of the Republic, the government has banned Islamic political groups, jailed religious leaders, and restricted freedoms. Though this policy has been temporarily effective in keeping Islam out of politics, it may fail in the long term. As Stephen Kinzer points out, "It has led many pious Muslims to conclude that the state despises religion and all who practice it, a conviction that feeds the fire of religious extremism rather than quenching it." He adds, "Those who govern Turkey . . . have given many Muslims the sense that they must choose between their religious faith and allegiance to the state. No state has ever prevailed in such a confrontation."[39]

The Welfare Party is Islamist, which means it wants Turkey to become an officially Muslim country that follows the law of the Koran. Welfare won 21 percent of the 1995 national election, more than any other party. Many Welfare mayors were elected throughout the country. Some supporters were not especially religious; rather, they were disgusted with the other politicians and wanted a change. Welfare promised honesty after years of government corruption, and peace and order after years of violence from terrorists and criminals. Party volunteers went directly to the voters and helped them in many ways, sheltering the homeless, feeding the hungry, and giving medicine to the sick. When people from the countryside came to the cities looking for work, Welfare helped them find jobs and places to stay. Once elected, many Welfare Party mayors focused on practical matters such as improving public transit and garbage collection.

In 1996, the Welfare Party's Necmettin Erbakan became prime minister. Erbakan wanted to take Turkey out of NATO and set up new versions of NATO, the United Nations, and the European Union with only Islamic countries as members. The military, which had backed Kemal's secular ideal from the start, forced Erbakan to resign and dissolved the Welfare Party for going against the constitutional ban on religion in politics. The political power of Islam has diminished since then. Some political groups do promote Islam, but they generally avoid making extreme demands.

Even those Turks who claim to want a modern, secular government often fear true democracy. The ruling politicians and military are afraid that if people are allowed to make their own decisions, they will make mistakes. They might choose Islamic rule, or communism, or other policies that would destroy Ataturk's Republican ideals. Many educated, worldly Turks agree that Turkey is not ready for true democracy. They fear the conflict that would come from people freely promoting different ideas. But Turkey will not be welcomed into the European Union while it puts so many restrictions on freedom.

ETHNIC RELATIONS
Turkey has laws against freedom of the press, speech, assembly, and religion. Laws have even prohibited people from

speaking a certain language or wearing certain clothes. One article of the Turkish constitution states: "Fundamental rights and freedoms may be restricted by law, in conformity with the letter and spirit of the Constitution, with the aim of safeguarding the indivisible integrity of the state with its territory and nation, national sovereignty, the Republic, national security, public order, general peace, the public interest, public morals and public health."[40] In other words, the government can limit people's freedom for just about any reason.

Ethnic minorities have suffered most from government repression. In the first half of the twentieth century, Greeks and Armenians were killed or sent out of Turkey. In recent decades, Kurds have been the victims of official government repression. About 20 percent of Turkey's people are Kurdish. Traditionally, Kurds were a tribal people who thought of themselves as members of their particular clan. Clans often warred against each other; sometimes one clan would help the government fight another. In the last few decades the idea of a Kurdish nationality grew, and with it the desire for a separate homeland in eastern Turkey.

Kurds are officially equal to Turks. A Kurd can reach the top level of success in any field, even politics—provided that he or she acts like a Turk. Kurdish language and culture are repressed, and anyone who promotes an independent Kurdish state—or even more rights for Kurds within Turkey—is considered an enemy of the government. Kurds who insist on keeping their culture usually are stuck in poverty. Most live in poor eastern villages with high rates of unemployment and a per capita income one-tenth that of the western provinces. Other Kurds have been forced to leave their homes and now live in ghettos on the edge of western cities.

Some Kurds resented their treatment so much that they turned against the government. Turkish Kurd historian Kendal Nezan claimed that "Repression has turned the Kurdish peasants into a race of outlaws."[41] The rebellious Kurdistan Workers Party, known as the PKK, began in the 1970s. A Kurd named Abdullah Ocalan led a band of rebels determined to make eastern Turkey an independent Kurdish state. His group quickly grew as young men and women joined guerilla fighters in the mountains. The PKK funded their war through heroin smuggling and foreign donations. Syria, which was fighting Turkey over water rights to the Eu-

SHOPPING IN TURKEY

The Grand Bazaar in Istanbul features more than four thousand shops in a labyrinth of covered passages. This tradition dates back to the early years of the Ottoman Empire, when such bazaars were the business center of every city. In *Everyday Life in Ottoman Turkey*, Raphaela Lewis describes the bazaar during Ottoman times: "There were lanes of carpet-sellers, of copper-smiths, of gold-beaters hammering the plates of metal into paper-thin leaves to be used in bookbinding and for precious inlays, and wire-workers who made untarnishable gold and silver trimmings for scabbards, saddles and ceremonial dress, sitting on the ground to draw the thread round the big toe, lanes of saddlers, druggists, cobblers . . . the list was endless."

Today tourists flood the bazaar to buy jewelry, leather goods, carpets, and trinkets. A shopkeeper will often invite a visitor in for tiny cups of strong Turkish coffee or sweet apple tea. The Egyptian Market is most famous for its spices, which are displayed in huge bags. Shops there also sell dried fruit, nuts, and candy. Local Turks generally shop in the back alleys and streets around the main bazaar. Many other streets throughout the city are lined with shops, from convenience stores to elegant fashion emporiums. Farmers' markets set up in a different part of the city each day, selling fruits, vegetables, and small household items from tables that line the street. In smaller towns, an open flea market may be the only shopping center, but in Istanbul a shopper can find just about anything, from traditional Turkish crafts to top-quality European imports.

Colorful ceramics line the walls of a shop at Istanbul's Grand Bazaar.

phrates River, gave the PKK money, weapons, and training bases. Groups in Russia, Greece, Armenia, and Iraq also lent support in hopes of weakening Turkey, their rival. In a few years, the PKK practically took over eastern Turkey. Many eastern locals supported the rebels, but the PKK also used

Kurdish rebels and Turkish police clash during a 1999 riot in Istanbul.

terror to maintain control. They assassinated Turkish school-teachers and doctors, as well as entire families of Kurds who seemed friendly to the army. The PKK even tortured and executed its own members if they disagreed with Ocalan.

CONTROLLING REBELLION

In the 1980s the Turkish government decided to take extreme measures to protect Turkey's stability. They banned the Kurdish political party and forced Kurd politicians from office. The army destroyed hundreds of eastern villages thought to be friendly to the PKK. Residents had one hour to gather their belongings and flee before soldiers set fire to their houses and crops. Government security agencies also hired assassins to kill civilians who backed the PKK. The only way the government saw to end the rebellion was to wipe out every thought of Kurdish nationalism. "The brutality of these tactics is indisputable," journalist Kinzer writes, "as is the brutality of the PKK's rebellion. . . . Turkey was facing a threat to its very existence as a unified state. . . . "[42]

By the end of the 1990s the army was in control again, though it suffered worldwide criticism for its brutal tactics. Ocalan offered to negotiate a cease-fire but the government refused to compromise. They captured him in 1999. The European Parliament, one of the governing bodies of the EU, wanted to hold an international conference to discuss the

Kurds. Turkey resented the interference. With the world watching they tried Ocalan, who admitted his crimes and stated, "Now is the time to end this conflict, or it will get much worse. I want to dedicate my life to bringing Kurds and Turks together."[43] Ocalan received the death sentence, but it was postponed. He remained a prisoner on an island in the Sea of Marmara, while the PKK guerillas either fled to Iraq or rejoined their families in Turkey. After two decades of fighting, the dead included twenty-three thousand Kurdish guerillas, five thousand Turkish soldiers, and nearly nine thousand civilians. Some two thousand villages were destroyed, leaving hundreds of thousands of people homeless.

Though the army won the war, they did not wipe out Kurdish nationalism. According to Kinzer, "Kurds emerged from the war with a greater sense of their own identity than ever before in their history. . . . Even those who did not support the rebellion have come to believe that there is such a thing as a Kurdish nation[al identity] and that they belong to it."[44] Most Kurds have given up the idea of actually establishing an independent Kurdish country, however. Now they just want peace and prosperity in Turkey, with the right to express their own culture. They want to be able to teach, publish, and broadcast freely in their own language. They also want to abolish the death penalty, primarily so Abdullah Ocalan and other Kurdish leaders cannot be executed. The European Union requires Turkey to make those changes anyway before it can join the EU.

Even though the government remains suspicious of all Kurds and has been slow to compromise, it has made some changes. The Kurdish political party came back with a new name and won many local elections in the southeast in 1999. Respected Turks, including novelists, university professors, and other intellectuals, are calling for more rights for Kurds. Two important judges called for major political reforms to improve Kurdish rights. One of them, Ahmet Necdet Sezer, was elected president of Turkey in May 2000.

The Turkish parliament has passed many reforms, including lifting the restrictions on speaking and publishing in Kurdish. They also passed laws that will give better rights to everyone living in Turkey, granting more freedom of association and more rights to privacy, while reducing the time people can be held in jail without being charged. Yet the Kurds have faced some setbacks. Students have been arrested for demanding the right to be taught in Kurdish, and suspected Kurdish nationalists have been murdered. If Turkey wants to move closer to Europe, it will have to solve this problem peacefully.

RICH SOIL, POOR PEOPLE

One way to make people happy and keep the country stable is to ensure that everyone has a comfortable lifestyle. This can be a major challenge, however. In the second half of the twentieth century, Turkey's agricultural output increased because of advances in machinery, fertilizer, and plant varieties. The wide range of climates and soil types throughout the country allows a variety of crops. Besides basics like wheat, barley, sugar beets, and lentils, Turkey grows many fruits and vegetables, nuts, olives, and specialty crops like tea and coffee. Cotton and tobacco are the biggest export crops.

However, the people who grow this rich food are among the poorest in Turkey. Almost 10 million people, over 40 percent of the labor force, work in agriculture. Yet farming earns only about 14 percent of the country's total income, and agricultural productivity has been falling in recent years. Many factors contribute to this problem, including inefficient small farms and a lack of organizations to help small farmers market their crops.

Turkey has tried to give its farmers an advantage by putting high taxes on imported goods, so Turkish products will be cheap in comparison. To join the EU, Turkey will need to stop that practice and allow free trade. They will also have to improve food safety and veterinary medicine. The EU helps some candidate countries by giving them money and resources to improve their agricultural production and safety. Turkey would like this help but the EU has been slow in giving it.

Turkey is also hoping to improve food production through the GAP/South Eastern Anatolia project. This large dam project, planned for completion by 2005, is drawing water from the rivers to irrigate more land. These hydroelectric dams will also supply much of Turkey's electricity. Along with the dams, the government is planning many social improvement projects for Southeastern Anatolia, such as land reform, health clinics, schools, and women's community centers.

THE STRUGGLE FOR STABILITY

Another problem facing Turkey is decades of high inflation. Inflation, a steady rise in prices, is normal in any economy. In most industrial countries, prices rise an average of less than 10 percent each year. However, in Turkey, the rate of inflation often has risen high above this average. For example, in the mid-1990s, Turkey's inflation rose as high as 150 percent. To counter this, Turkey sold state-owned businesses to private companies and raised the prices of products sold from the businesses they retained.

Turkey's inflation rates fell during the year 2000, but an economic setback in 2001 dashed hopes for an inflation rate below 10 percent. Prices continue to rise rapidly, and wages may not keep up. Turkey's overall economy has grown over the years. But because its population also has increased, individual incomes do not necessarily reflect this growth. Right now the per capita income (average yearly

Two Turkish girls pose in a tobacco field. Although tobacco and cotton are Turkey's biggest exports, the people who grow them are among the country's poorest residents.

wages and benefits per person) is about $3,000, compared to about $30,000 in the United States.

Turkey must solve its economic problems before the European Union will welcome it. The government has made many plans to reduce inflation and improve the economy. They have considered laws to reform retirement pension funds and to better regulate the banking sector. They want to encourage foreign companies to invest in Turkey, as well as to export more Turkish products to other countries. They want to strengthen telecommunications and transportation in order to better support other businesses so that they may compete in the modern age. The government also hopes to expand the economy in areas such as tourism.

ATTRACTING TOURISTS

Turkey's expansive and beautiful beaches are among the country's most attractive tourist destinations.

As a tourist destination, Turkey has many attractions—beautiful beaches for swimming, fishing, and boating; snowy mountains for winter sports; lively cities; and millennia of history showcased in ruins, historic buildings, and

museums. Turkey has tried to lure tourists by improving these sites. Many Ottoman palaces and homes have been restored as tourist destinations. Guests can feel like sultans at five-star hotels that offer a combination of Ottoman splendor and modern conveniences. Tourism authorities are trying to improve roads, water, electricity, and the training of hotel and tour personnel. They also are developing alternative attractions such as camping, bird watching, hunting, golf, and religious tourism.

As a result, tourism has become a major part of the Turkish economy. In 1997, 9.8 million tourists brought revenues equal to 7 billion U.S. dollars to Turkey. About 1 million people work in Turkey's tourism industry, and some sixty-five thousand students are trained in tourism schools yearly. Tourism usually does not require a high level of education, and it encourages the development of small businesses such as hotels and sight-seeing companies. Tourism also brings ordinary Turks closer to Europe, because they get to know foreign visitors and may even learn their languages.

Unfortunately, tourism has suffered a series of setbacks that discourage visitors. In 1999, the capture and trial of PKK leader Abdullah Ocalan gave some tourists a bad impression of Turkey, since many Europeans and Americans sympathized with the Kurds. Then in August 1999, a major earthquake hit northwestern Turkey. Not only did the quake claim over seventeen thousand lives and cause large economic losses, but foreigners started to think Turkey was a dangerous place to go. The terrorist attacks in America on September 11, 2001, increased that feeling; many Westerners assumed the entire Middle East was dangerous for Americans and Europeans.

Yet according to the World Travel & Tourism Council, Turkey is expected to be the fastest growing country in the world for travel and tourism, with a growth rate of over 10 percent per year until 2010. That will depend partly on Turkey's ability to convince visitors that it is a safe place to stay. Turkey is trying to distance itself from some of its war-torn Middle Eastern neighbors, and build its reputation as a modern, safe country.

Nature At Risk

By the late 1980s Turkey had become a popular Mediterranean holiday spot, with many visitors coming from northern Europe on package tours. Unfortunately, this growth came at the expense of the environment. The natural resources that drew visitors to Turkey were damaged and polluted by those visitors. Zürcher writes, "Turkey went in for low to medium budget mass tourism and large parts of its coasts were commercialized and covered with areas of hotels, holiday villages and resorts identical to those in Spain, Greece and Cyprus with which it competed mainly on price."[45]

In the short term, Turkey succeeded in drawing more tourists. But because Turkey put economic growth ahead of environmental protection, some natural attractions were devastated. In fact, some beach resorts no longer allow swimming because the water is so badly polluted. To continue to attract tourists from around the world, Turkey must protect its beautiful natural resources. Turkey's varied environment, with lush coastlines, arid plateaus, and high mountains, contains an enormous number of plant species. Of the approximately twelve thousand species of European flora, about three-quarters grow in Turkey. Fevzi Aytekin, Turkey's environment minister, claims, "Turkey has a unique geographic and geopolitical situation, a junction of old civilisations and beautiful nature, which we would like to share with Europe."[46]

Turkey must make some changes before it can do that as an official member of the EU. According to Pavel Antonov of the Regional Environmental Center for Central and Eastern Europe, "The European Commission's 2000 report on Turkey's progress towards accession [to the EU] lists several areas where the country must improve its environmental performance, including: air quality, waste management, water quality, nature protection, industrial pollution control and risk management, use of genetically modified organisms and nuclear safety."[47]

The Bosporus Strait is one area that is getting a lot of attention. Up to forty-five thousand ships pass through the Bosporus each year. Oil tanker accidents there have spilled huge loads of oil into the Black and Marmara Seas, threatening marine life. Authorities are trying to reduce the risk with

Cotton Castle

About one hundred miles from the Aegean coast in western Turkey, a rounded white cliff rises 330 feet from the surrounding plain. Pamukkale (pam-uck-al-lay) means "cotton castle," and legend claims the formation is hardened cotton, left out to dry by giants. In reality, a warm volcanic spring at the top of the cliff pours mineral-rich water over natural terraces. The calcium in the water slowly solidifies into formations that have been compared to white curtains and frozen frosting.

The thermal springs have drawn visitors for more than twenty-three centuries. The ancient city of Hierapolis was founded in 190 B.C. on the hill above the white cliffs. Hierapolis was famous for its sacred healing waters, believed to cure rheumatism and other ailments. The city reached its peak in the second and third centuries A.D. The remains of a theater and temples from that era have been partially reconstructed.

In the 1990s, the springs were diverted into the swimming pools of nearby luxury hotels. Thousands of visitors tramped over the white cliffs and soaked in basins there. Soon the cotton cliffs turned a dingy gray.

Now most sections are off-limits, and visitors must walk barefoot over the one open pathway. The mineralized water is directed over different sections of the cliff to slowly whiten them. Hotels must now fill their pools with regular city water, although tourists can still swim among broken Roman columns in the ancient Sacred Pool on top of the cliffs. The water stays about 95 degrees Fahrenheit and contains minerals and a high level of natural radioactivity.

The cotton castle of Pamukkale has attracted visitors for over 2,300 years.

a new navigation system that uses computers and satellites to control shipping traffic. Over-fishing has also hurt the Black Sea by reducing the number of fish that can be found there. In addition, businesses have been accused of dumping pollutants into the sea and into inland water sources. Even the dams being built in southeastern Turkey have some people worried. Though meant to improve agriculture and energy, some people fear that the dams will pollute the water supply as people dump untreated waste into the rivers.

Some Turks are joining environmental groups such as Greenpeace to demand protection for nature. Turkey has seen that tourism can help the economy but that poor planning can destroy the natural resources needed to draw tourists. New plans must consider how best to prevent environmental damage while increasing economic gains.

A PLACE IN THE MIDDLE

Throughout the last century, the Turkish government has tried to modernize Turkey through a series of small and large changes. In 1928, an editorial in the newspaper *Cumhuriyet* reflected on the change from Arabic script to a Latin alphabet. "As a result of our revolutionary change of script, our dear Turkey looks completely like Europe. In less than one year it will have the true key of civilization and knowledge in its hand."[48]

Despite that prediction, the change has been slow, and many Turks today do not want to entirely lose their Middle Eastern side. Orhan Pamuk, one of Turkey's leading novelists, says, "Turkey is constantly moving toward Europe, becoming more Westernized. But a union will never be realized. Turkey's place is in continuous flux. This limbo is what Turkey is and will stay forever. This is our way of life here."[49]

If Turkey does meet the EU's standards for admission, the rewards will include greater freedom for all citizens as well as better financial opportunities. The benefits will also extend beyond the country itself. Europe and the Middle East will also gain from having a strong meeting point, a place that bridges the gap between East and West, Islam and Christianity, traditional tribal society and modern democracy. Turkey could become an example of democracy for other Islamic countries, encouraging them to forge ties with the Western world. Turkey could also show Europe that a Muslim country can be a friend and ally, not a threat.

"Once again," Kinzer says, "as during the Ottoman centuries, it would stand like a colossus at the point where two continents come together, drawing riches from both and offering itself as a meeting point for civilizations that might otherwise drift toward calamitous confrontation."[50]

FACTS ABOUT TURKEY

GEOGRAPHY

Area: 301,380 square miles (780,580 square kilometers)

Bordering countries: Greece, Bulgaria (northwest); Georgia, Armenia, Azerbaijan (northeast); Iran, Iraq, Syria (southeast)

GOVERNMENT

Full name: Turkiye Cumhuriyeti (Republic of Turkey)

Capital: Ankara

Government type: Republican parliamentary democracy

President: Ahmet Necdet Sezer (since May 16, 2000)

Prime Minister: Bulent Ecevit (since January 11, 1999)

Elections: The president is elected by the National Assembly for a seven-year term. The prime minister is appointed by the president.

Cabinet: A Council of Ministers is nominated by the prime minister and appointed by the president; the National Security Council serves as an advisory group.

PEOPLE

Population (July 2001): Approximately 66,493,970

Ethnic groups: Turkish, 80 percent; Kurdish, 20 percent

Principal languages: Turkish (official), Kurdish, Arabic, Armenian, and Greek

Literacy rate (2000): 85 percent (total population); 94 percent (male)

Life expectancy (2002): Female, 73.71 years; male, 68.89 years

Religion: Over 99 percent Islamic

ECONOMY

Monetary unit: Turkish lira

Exchange Rate (2002): Turkish liras per U.S. dollar–1,223,140.

Labor force (2000): 23 million; agriculture, 38 percent; services, 38 percent; industry, 24 percent

Chief products: tobacco, cotton, grain, olives, sugar beets, pulses, citrus fruits, livestock, textiles, food processing, autos, petroleum, lumber, construction, mining (coal, copper, chromite, boron), steel, paper

Chief exports: apparel, foodstuffs, textiles, metal manufactures, transport equipment

Export partners (2000): Germany, 18.7 percent; United States, 11.4 percent; UK, 7.4 percent; Italy, 6.3 percent; France, 6.0 percent

NOTES

INTRODUCTION: CROSSROADS OF CULTURES

1. Dana Facaros and Michael Pauls, *Cadogan Turkey*. London: Cadogan Guides, 2000, p. 50.

CHAPTER 1: WHERE CONTINENTS COLLIDE

2. Lynn Levine, *Frommer's Turkey*. New York: IDG Books Worldwide, 2000, p. 157.

3. Jacky ter Horst-Meijer (translator from the Dutch), *Turkey hos geldiniz!* London: Edu'Actief Publishing, 1990, p. 6.

4. Quoted in Harry Rutstein and Joanne Kroll, *In the Footsteps of Marco Polo: A Twentieth-Century Odyssey*. New York: The Viking Press, 1980, p. 65.

5. Facaros and Pauls, *Cadogan Turkey*, p. 492.

CHAPTER 2: THE PASSING OF EMPIRES

6. Roderic H. Davison, *Turkey*. Englewood Cliffs, NJ: Prentice-Hall, 1968, p. 17.

7. Davison, *Turkey*, p. 22.

8. Quoted in Davison, *Turkey*, p. 22.

9. Davison, *Turkey*, p. 40.

10. Douglas A. Howard, *The History of Turkey*. Westport, CT: Greenwood Press, 2001, p. 40.

11. Quoted in Davison, *Turkey*, p. 28.

12. Quoted in Davison, *Turkey*, p. 47.

13. Noel Barber, *The Sultans*. New York: Simon and Schuster, 1973, p. 61.

14. Tom Brosnahan, *Istanbul*. Victoria, Australia: Lonely Planet Publications, 1999, p. 16.

15. Quoted in Barber, *The Sultans*, p. 116.

16. Quoted in Nicole Pope and Hugh Pope, *Turkey Unveiled:*

A History of Modern Turkey. Woodstock, NY: The Overlook Press, 1998, p. 40.

17. Barber, *The Sultans,* p. 203.

18. Pope and Pope, *Turkey Unveiled,* p. 33.

CHAPTER 3: THE REPUBLIC

19. Quoted in Barber, *The Sultans,* p. 230.

20. Quoted in Pope and Pope, *Turkey Unveiled,* p. 45

21. Brosnahan, *Istanbul,* 1999, p. 17.

22. Quoted in Howard, *The History of Turkey,* p. 89.

23. Davison, *Turkey,* p.127.

24. Erik J. Zürcher, *Turkey: A Modern History.* London: I.B. Tauris, 1998, p. 180.

25. Zürcher, *Turkey,* p. 192.

26. Pope and Pope, *Turkey Unveiled,* p. 51.

27. Howard, *The History of Turkey,* p. 186.

CHAPTER 4: DAILY LIFE

28. Brosnahan, *Istanbul,* p. 162.

29. Stephen Kinzer, *Crescent & Star: Turkey Between Two Worlds.* New York: Farrar, Straus and Giroux, 2001, p. 179.

30. "Defense and Security," found at the Embassy of the Republic of Turkey in Washington, DC. www.turkey.org.

31. Pope and Pope, *Turkey Unveiled,* p. 305.

CHAPTER 5: ARTS AND ENTERTAINMENT

32. Brosnahan, *Istanbul,* p. 21.

33. Brosnahan, *Istanbul,* p. 21.

34. Mary Lee Settle, *Turkish Reflections: A Biography of a Place.* New York: Prentice-Hall Press, 1991, p. 53.

35. Horst-Meijer, *Turkey hos geldiniz!,* p. 135.

36. Brosnahan, *Istanbul,* p. 158.

37. Brosnahan, *Istanbul,* p. 22.

CHAPTER 6: TODAY'S CHALLENGES

38. Kinzer, *Crescent & Star,* p. 22.

39. Kinzer, *Crescent & Star*, pp. 60–61.

40. Quoted in Kinzer, *Crescent & Star*, p. 14.

41. Quoted in Pope and Pope, *Turkey Unveiled*, p. 258.

42. Kinzer, *Crescent & Star*, p. 113.

43. Quoted in Kinzer, *Crescent & Star*, p. 126.

44. Kinzer, *Crescent & Star*, p. 118.

45. Zürcher, *Turkey*, p. 318.

46. Quoted in Pavel Antonov, "Turkey's natural wealth meets with new pressures," *Candidate Country Focus*, The Regional Environmental Center for Central and Eastern Europe. http://bulletin.rec.org.

47. Antonov, "Turkey's natural wealth meets with new pressures."

48. Quoted in Pope and Pope, *Turkey Unveiled*, p. 180.

49. Quoted in Pope and Pope, *Turkey Unveiled*, p. 180.

50. Kinzer, *Crescent & Star*, p. 25.

CHRONOLOGY

8000–5000 B.C.
People settle in villages during the New Stone Age era.

1650–1200
Hittites conquer most of what is now Turkey.

Ca. 1000
Greek colonists begin settling along Turkey's western coast.

550–334
The Persian Empire controls Turkey.

334–333
Alexander the Great invades Anatolia.

133–66
Rome takes over Anatolia.

A.D. 476–1453
Constantinople is the capital of the Byzantine Empire.

1078
Islamic Seljuk warriors control most of Anatolia and are near Constantinople.

1290–1300
The Turkoman leader Osman founds the Ottoman Empire.

1520–1566
The Ottoman Empire reaches its political and cultural height during the reign of Sultan Suleiman the Magnificent.

1875
After borrowing money from Europe, the Ottoman Empire goes bankrupt; France, England, and Germany demand reforms.

1878
Serbia, Bulgaria, and Romania gain independence; In response to ongoing rebellions by Armenia, Crete, and Macedonia, Sultan Abdul Hamit II orders the slaughter of Armenians throughout the Empire.

1914–1918
The "Triple Alliance" of Austria-Hungary, Germany, and Italy fight together against the "Entente Powers" of Russia, France, and England in World War I; Turkey backs Germany.

1915 April–1916 January
British and Turkish forces battle at Gallipoli; the British withdraw on January 9.

1918
The Ottoman government signs the Armistice of Mudros to end World War I; British, French, and Italian troops occupy Anatolia, and Armenia is declared independent.

1919–1922
Mustafa Kemal leads the Turkish War of Independence.

1923
The Republic of Turkey is formed. Ankara becomes the new capital and the Assembly elects Mustafa Kemal as its first president.

1938
Mustafa Kemal dies.

1939–1945
World War II is fought across Europe; Turkey declares war against Germany and Japan in 1945.

1952
Turkey becomes a member of NATO, the North Atlantic Treaty Organization.

1974
Turkey invades northern Cyprus.

1978–1999
The Kurdistan Workers Party (PKK) fights for Kurdish independence.

1987
Turkey applies for candidacy in the European Union but is not accepted.

1999 August
A major earthquake in northwestern Turkey kills over seventeen thousand people.

1999 December
Turkey is given candidate status in the European Union.

FOR FURTHER READING

BOOKS

Noel Barber, *The Sultans*. New York: Simon and Schuster, 1973. History that reads like a novel, following the Ottoman Empire from the reign of Sultan Suleiman to the rise of Mustafa Kemal.

Charles Clark, *Islam* (Religions of the World Series). San Diego: Lucent Books, 2001. Explains the beliefs and practices of Muslims.

John Dunn, *The Spread of Islam* (World History Series). San Diego: Lucent Books, 1996. A detailed history of Islam.

Matthew S. Gordon, *Islam: Origins, Practices, Holy Texts, Sacred Persons, Sacred Places*. New York: Oxford University Press, 2002. A balanced introduction to Islam, with color photographs and illustrations.

Stephen Kinzer, *Crescent & Star: Turkey Between Two Worlds*. New York: Farrar, Straus and Giroux, 2001. Kinzer clearly loves Turkey yet understands its flaws. He presents the challenges Turkey faces, with lively anecdotes from modern and historical Turkish life.

Natasha Lesser, ed., *Fodor's Turkey*. New York: Fodor's Travel Publications, 1999. This travel guide brings the sights of Turkey to life.

Raphaela Lewis, *Everyday Life in Ottoman Turkey*. New York: G.P. Putnams Sons, 1971. An entertaining read on Ottoman life, with imagined scenes from the slave market to the sultan's palace.

John Miller and Kirsten Miller, eds., *Chronicles Abroad: Istanbul*. San Francisco: Chronicles Books, 1995. A collection of writings by various Turks and travelers to Turkey, both recent and historical.

William Spencer, *The Land and People of Turkey*. New York: J.B. Lippincott, 1990. Provides a good overview of Turkish culture, especially daily life and the arts.

Thomas Streissguth, *The Transcaucasus*. San Diego: Lucent Books, 2001. Covers the history of Armenia, including the influence of the Turks.

John F. Wukovits, *World War I: Strategic Battles*. San Diego: Lucent Books, 2002. Describes the battle of Gallipoli and explains its importance to World War I.

WEBSITES

All About Turkey (www.balsoy.com). This directory from the Turkish Ministry of Foreign Affairs provides links to online resources offering everything Turkish, from recipes to music to language guides to poetry (some in Turkish, some in English).

Central Intelligence Agency (www.cia.gov). The U.S. CIA provides facts on the Turkish government, economy, military, and international issues.

Embassy of the Republic of Turkey, Washington, D.C. (www.turkey.org). This official Turkish Embassy site provides news, plus a country profile and information on the government,economy, art, and culture.

Turkish Daily News(www.turkishdailynews.com). Turkey's largest online English-language newspaper.

Turkish Odyssey(www.turkishodyssey.com). The online site of "The first guide book of Turkey ever written by a Turk" discusses geography, history, mythology, and places of interest, with photos and maps.

WORKS CONSULTED

BOOKS

Ugur Ayyildiz, *All of Istanbul*. Istanbul, Turkey: Net Turistik Yayinlar A.S., 1995, 2000. Brief descriptions of sights in Istanbul, with plenty of color pictures.

Arin Bayraktaroglu, *Culture Shock! Turkey: A Guide to Customs and Etiquette*. Portland, OR: Graphic Arts Center Publishing Company, 2000. Explains the habits and attitudes particular to Turkey.

Tom Brosnahan, *Istanbul*. Victoria, Australia: Lonely Planet Publications, 1999. An entertaining guidebook to Istanbul, with information about Turkish history, arts, and culture.

Roderic H. Davison, *Turkey*. Englewood Cliffs, NJ: Prentice-Hall, 1968. A history of Turkey by an expert on the country, focusing especially on the twentieth century.

J.C. Dewdney, *Turkey: An Introductory Geography*. New York: Praeger Publishers, 1971. Provides an in-depth look at the geographical regions of Turkey.

Dana Facaros and Michael Pauls, *Cadogan Turkey*. London: Cadogan Guides, 2000. A guidebook with a brief, clear history of Turkey and entertaining essays on unique aspects of Turkish life.

Brian M. Fagan, ed., *Eyewitness to Discovery: First-Person Accounts of More Than Fifty of the World's Greatest Archaeological Discoveries*. New York: Oxford University Press, 1996. Includes essays on Heinrich Schliemann's discovery of Troy.

Michael M. Gunter, *The Kurds and the Future of Turkey*. New York: St. Martin's Press, 1997. A thoughtful analysis of the Kurdish struggle with suggestions for a solution.

Jacky ter Horst-Meijer (translator from the Dutch), *Turkey hos geldiniz!: Welcome to the Cultures of Asia Minor.* London: Edu' Actief Publishing, 1990. This book divides Turkey into historical regions and gives a history of each, with photos and sidebars on Turkish culture.

Douglas A. Howard, *The History of Turkey.* Westport, CT: Greenwood Press, 2001. A history of Turkey concentrating on the twentieth century.

Lynn Levine, *Frommer's Turkey.* New York: IDG Books Worldwide, 2000. A travel guide with poetic descriptions of the sights of Turkey.

Seton Lloyd, *Ancient Turkey: A Traveller's History of Anatolia.* Berkeley, CA: University of California Press, 1989. Explores archaeological landmarks from prehistoric times to the Christian era, with an emphasis on the fascinating people who changed history.

Nicole Pope and Hugh Pope, *Turkey Unveiled: A History of Modern Turkey.* Woodstock, NY: The Overlook Press, 1998. An analytical account of Turkish history, focusing on the twentieth century.

Harry Rutstein and Joanne Kroll, *In the Footsteps of Marco Polo: A Twentieth-Century Odyssey.* New York: The Viking Press, 1980. The authors include excerpts from Marco Polo's journals alongside their own travel experience in Turkey and other parts of the Silk Road.

Mary Lee Settle, *Turkish Reflections: A Biography of a Place.* New York: Prentice-Hall Press, 1991. Personal essays reflect on the author's travels through Turkey.

Eric Solsten, ed., *Cyprus, a Country Study.* Washington, DC: Federal Research Division, Library of Congress, Government Printing Office, 1993. Explains Turkey's claims to the island of Cyprus.

Erik J. Zürcher, *Turkey: A Modern History.* London: I.B. Tauris, 1998. A political history of Turkey from 1789–1991.

INDEX

Abduction from the Seraglio (opera), 79
Academy of Fine Arts, 76
Aegean coast, 12–14
Aegean Sea, 10–11, 12
agriculture
  in Central Anatolia, 16–17
  in Cyprus, 20
  in Fertile Crescent, 20
  increase in, 90
  near Black Sea coast, 15
  in Turkish Thrace, 10
Ahmet I, 24
Aladdin, 73
alcohol, 56–57
Alexander the Great, 24–25
Alexius, 26
Allah, 56
alphabet, 50, 77
Amazon warriors, 14, 17
Anatolia, 29–30, 42, 45
Anatolian Peninsula, 9, 10, 47
  See also Asia Minor
Ankara, 17, 46–47, 49
Antony, Marc, 12–13
ANZAC. *see* Australian–New Zealand
  Army Corps
Arabian Nights, The, 73
Arabic script, 50, 77
architecture, 70–72
Aristotle, 31
Armenia, 9, 36, 46
Armenians
  clothing worn by, 63
  killing of, 36–38, 41–42, 86
  population of, 42
art(s)
  Islamic, 69–70, 72
  decorative, 72–73
  visual, 75–76
Asia Minor, 9, 25, 41, 46
Asklepion, 13
Atatürk, 52
Australian–New Zealand Army Corps (AN-
  ZAC), 44–45
Austria-Hungary, 41
Aya Sofya, 24, 32
Azerbaijan, 9

Balkan Peninsula, 10
Basil, Saint, 18
bathing, 37, 71
Bayezid, 28
bazaars, 87
belly dancing, 81–82
Bergama, 12, 13
Beyoglu, 11
birth ceremonies, 58–60
Black Sea, 10, 95
  coast, 14–15
Blue Mosque, 24
boating, 14
Bosporus Strait, 10, 11, 41, 94–95
breakfast, 58

Britain
  control of Cyprus, 53
  control of Turkey, 46
  role at Gallipoli, 11, 43–45
Bulgaria, 10, 35, 36
burial rituals, 68
Byzantine Empire, 11
Byzantine period, 25–26
Byzantine-style domes, 71
Byzantium, 11

caftans, 63
calendar, European, 49
calligraphy, 72
Cappadocia, 17–18, 70
caravans, 15
carpets, 74–75
cave churches, 18
cave homes, 17–18
cave hotels, 18
Cemal, 40
censorship, 30, 50, 53, 54, 78, 81, 84, 89
Central Anatolia, 15–17, 26
ceramic tile, 72–73
Ceremonial Hall, 71
childhood
  ceremonies during, 58–60
  education during, 60
  youth activities, 60–62
Children's Day, 59
Christian Crusaders, 26
Ciller, Tansu, 67
circumcision, 59–60
cirit matches, 61
cities
  ancient, 20
  underground, 17–18
  lifestyles in, 7, 56–57, 59, 60
civil code, 49
Cleopatra (queen of Egypt), 12–13
clothing, 50, 63
coal mining, 15
Committee of Union and Progress, 38
concubines, 32, 35
Constantine the Great, 24
Constantinople, 11, 25, 29
  see also Istanbul
constitution, 34, 54, 86
convents, 18
copper mining, 20–21
corruption, 33
cotton castle, 95
courtship rituals, 65
Crete, 36
criminal code, 49
cuisine, Turkish, 58
currency, 48, 83
Cyprus, 20–21, 53–54

dams, 90
dance, 80–82
Dardanelles, 11, 12, 42, 47
death, 68

decorative arts, 72–73
democracy
  description of, 83–84
  fear of, 85
  introduction of, 6–7, 39
  significance of, 96
Democratic Party, 53
dervishes, 81
dinner, 58
divorce, 66
Dolmabahce Palace, 71
droughts, 16
dyes, carpet, 75

Eastern Highlands, 18–19
Eastern Roman Empire, 25–26
economy, 91–92, 93
education, 39, 60
Egypt, 36
Egyptian Market, 87
engagement parties, 65
England, 34, 41
Entente powers
  agreement among, 46
  attack at Gallipoli, 42–45
  countries in, 41
  occupation of Turkey, 46–47
  seize control of Dardanelles, 42
  wartime casualties, 45
Enver, 40, 41, 45
environmental protection, 94–96
Ephesus, 13–14, 37, 70
Erbakan, Necmettin, 85
ethnic Kurds, 42
ethnic minorities, 86
ethnic nationalism, 34
eunuchs, 35
Euphrates River, 19, 20
euro, 83
European Parliament, 88
European Union (EU), 83, 88–89, 90, 92

fairy chimneys, 17
farming, 90
fasting, 56, 57
Fertile Crescent, 19–20
fez, 50, 63
First Crusade, 26
fishing, 14
floral designs, 72, 74
folk dances, 80–81
folksongs, 80
folktales, 78
food, Turkish, 58
food safety, 90
France, 34, 40, 41
Franz Ferdinand (archduke of Austria-
  Hungary), 41
free trade, 90

Galland, Antoine, 73
Gallipoli, Battle of, 11, 42–45
GAP/South Eastern Anatolia project, 90
Garden of Eden, 20
Gauls, 25
Gelibolu Peninsula Historical National
  Park, 11
Genghis Khan, 26
geography
  Aegean coast, 12–14
  Black Sea coast, 14–15
  Cappadocia, 17–18
  Central Anatolia, 15–17

Eastern Highlands, 18–19
Fertile Crescent, 19–20
Istanbul, 11
location and boundaries, 9–10
map of Turkey, 10
Mediterranean coast, 14
North Cyprus, 20–21
Turkish Thrace, 10–11
geometric designs, 72, 74
George, Saint, 18
Georgia, 9
Germany, 34, 40–41, 53
Ghazis, 29
Golden Horn, 11
government
  army takeover of, 54
  during early 1900s, 39–40
  first president of, 49
  future of, 83–85
  Kemalism, 49–54
  reform measures, 49
  after World War II, 53
  see also democracy
Grand Bazaar, 87
Grand National Assembly, 49
grand vizier, 29, 33
Greece, 10, 42, 47–49
Greeks
  Christian, 34
  clothing worn by, 63
  empire created by, 24–25
  living in Cyprus, 53–54
  living in Turkey, 42, 48–49
  move back to Greece, 42, 48–49
  repression of, 86
  settlements of, 23
Gulf War, 54

hamams, 37
Hamid, 40
Hamilton, Ian, 44, 45
Hamit II, Abdul, 34–38
harems, 32, 33, 35
Hattusa, 22
Hazivad, 82
Hercules, 14
Hierapolis, 95
hiking, 15
Hikmet, Nazim, 81
historic preservation, 71
Hittites, 17, 18, 20, 22–23
Hoca, Nasrettin, 78
homework, 61
Huns, 26
hygiene, 37

infant mortality rates, 68
inflation, 91–92
Iran, 9
Iraq, 10
Islam
  boy's admission into, 59
  brought to Turkey, 6, 26
  cultural influence of, 26, 57
  followers of, 56
  political power of, 85
  Turks' conversion to, 30
Islamic art, 69–70, 72
Islamic law, 6, 30, 50
Istanbul
  becomes capital, 29
  Grand Bazaar in, 87
  historic sites in, 24
  history of, 11

rebels' control over, 47
rebuilding of, 30
tourist sites in, 24, 87
Istanbul House of Detention (poem), 81
Italian criminal code, 49
Italy, 41
Izmir, 12

Japan, 53
Jason and the Argonauts, 14
Jews, 42, 63
John, Saint, 13
Justinian, 24

Karagoz, 82
Kemal, Mustafa
  becomes president, 49
  becomes Turkish hero, 45
  birthday celebration of, 59
  principles of, 49–50
  reform measures by, 6, 50–52
  role at Gallipoli, 44–45
  sets up rebel government, 46–47
Kemal, Yashar, 77–78
Kemalism, 49–52
khans, 15
Koran, the, 29, 72, 85
Kurdish nationalism, 86–87, 88–90
Kurdistan Workers Party (PKK), 86–89
Kurds
  ethnic, 19
  legal rights of, 86
  nationalist movement by, 86–87, 88–90
  rebellion by, 50
  repression of, 50

laws, 85–86
library, 12–13
life expectancy, 68
lira, 48, 83
literature, 76–78
lunch, 58

Macedonia, 24, 36
Mahmud II, 63
Mahomet V, 38
Marco Polo, 14, 18
marriage, 65–66
Mausoleum of Halicarnassus, 70
meals, 58
Mecca, 68
medical center, 13
Mediterranean coast, 14
Mehmed I, 28–29
Mehmed II, 24, 29–30
Mehmed VI, 46–47, 49
Mehmed, My Hawk (Kemal), 77
midwives, 59
military, 29
Military Governor of Constantinople, 40
military service, 62, 64
Minister of Marine, 40
Minister of the Interior, 40
Ministry of Culture, 75
monasticism, 18
Mongols, 26–27
monks, 81
mosques, 71
mountains
  near Black Sea coast, 14–15
  in Eastern Highlands, 18
  near Mediterranean coast, 14
  see also names of specific mountains
Mount Ararat, 18

movies, 61
Mozart, Wolfgang Amadeus, 79
Mt. Erciyes, 15
muezzin, 68
Muhammad, 26, 56
Munro, Charles, 45
music, 78–80
Muslims, 56–57, 63

Nationalism, 50
National Pact, 46
National Youth and Sports Day, 59
natural resources, 94–96
newspapers, 53
New Stone Age, 22
Nobel Prize for Literature, 77
nomads, 19, 26
North Atlantic Treaty Organization
  (NATO), 53, 85
North Cyprus, 20–21
novels, 77

Ocalan, Abdullah, 86, 88–89, 93
oil wrestling, 61
Old Stone Age, 22
Oriental dance, 81–82
Oryantal, 81–82
Osman, 27–28
Ottoman Empire
  capital of, 11
  clothing worn during, 63
  collapse of, 38, 46
  deterioration of, 33–38
  division of, 46
  founding of, 27
  geographical expansion during, 29–30,
    30–33
  Greeks living in Turkey during, 42
  lifestyle during, 6, 30, 34
  map of, 27
  power struggles during, 28–29
  travel during, 15
  during World War I, 45–46
Ottomanization, 39
Ottoman Painter's Society, 76
Özal, Turgut, 54

Pamuk, Orhan, 77, 96
parchment paper, 12
parliament, 34–35, 38
Paul, Saint, 13
People's Houses, 70
Pergamum, 12, 13, 25
Persian armies, 23
PKK. *See* Kurdistan Workers Party
poetry, 76, 81
pollution, 95
Populism, 49
pottery, 72
prayer, 56, 68
prayer carpets, 75
pregnancy, 59
preservation, historic, 71
president, 54
prime minister, 54
public baths, 37, 71

rafting, white-water, 15
Ramadan, 56, 57
religion, 50
  see also Islam; Muslims
Republicanism, 49
Revolutionism, 50
rights, individual

under Hamit II, 34–35
for non-Muslims, 30
for women, 30, 65, 66–67
see also censorship
Roman Empire, 11, 25
Romania, 35
Rome, 25
Roxelana, 32
rural areas
childbirth in, 59
clothing worn in, 63
lifestyle in, 7
religion in, 19, 57
schools in, 60
songs and dances in, 80
women in, 66
youth activities in, 61
Russia, 40, 41

Sanliurfa, 20
Scheherazade, 73
School of Fine Arts for Women, 76
schools, 39, 57, 60
Sea of Marmara, 10–11, 12
Secularism, 50
Selim, 32–33
Seljuks, 26–27
Serbia, 35, 36
Seven Wonders of the World, 70
Sezer, Ahmet Necdet, 55, 89
Shadow Play and Traditional Turkish The-
ater Contest, 82
shadow-puppet theater, 82
Shakespeare, William, 82
shamanistic religions, 26
shopping, 87
Silk Road, 14
Sinan, Mimar, 71
Sinbad the Sailor, 73
skiing, 15, 19
slaves, 32, 35
smoking, 57
soldiers, 29, 33
soldiers, drafted, 62, 64
Spanish Inquisition, 42
sports, 14, 61–62
Stamboul, 11, 24, 35
State Opera and Ballet Company, 82
Statism, 49–50
steel mills, 15
Suleiman, 30–33, 71
Suleiman's Mosque, 71
Sultanahmet Mosque, 24
sultans, origins of, 26
Sumerians, 20
Swiss civil code, 49
Syria, 10

Talaat, 40, 42, 45
Tamerlane, 28
teenagers, 62, 64
Temple of Artemis, 70
theater, 82
Thousand and One Nights, The, 73
Tigris River, 19, 20
tiles, building, 72–73
toilets, 37
Topkapi Palace, 35, 79
tourism
on Aegean coast, 13
belly dancing and, 82

in Cappadocia, 18
exchange rates and, 48
at Hierapolis, 95
industry, 92–94
in Istanbul, 24, 87
on Mediterranean coast, 14
Turkish-made items and, 73, 75, 87
trade routes
in Anatolia, 16
caravan stops along, 15
near Constantinople, 34
through Dardanelles, 11
along Silk Road, 14
during World War I, 41
Treaty of Sèvres, 47
Triple Alliance, 41
turbans, 63
Turkish Armed Forces, 62, 64
Turkish carpets, 74–75
Turkish Cypriots, 20, 53–54
Turkish language, 40
Turkish Republic of North Cyprus, 20–21
Turkish Riviera, 14
Turkish Thrace, 10–11, 47
Turkish War of Independence, 42
Turkism, ideal of, 39–40
Turkoman soldiers, 29
Turkoman tribe, 26
TV, 61, 82

uniforms, school, 60
United Nations, 53, 54
United States, 53, 54
urban lifestyles, 7, 56–57, 59, 60
Uskudar, 11
USSR (Russia), 53

veils, 63
veterinary medicine, 90
video games, 61
virginity, 66
visual arts, 75–76

warfare, 29
War Minister, 40
water sports, 14
weddings, 65
Welfare Party, 85
Western Roman Empire, 25
whirling dervishes, 81
women
Armenian, 41
belly dancing by, 82
carpets made by, 74
clothing worn by, 50
in harems, 33, 35
opportunities for, 39
rights of, 30, 65, 66–67
veils worn by, 63
in workforce, 67
World War I
Battle of Gallipoli, 11, 42–45
casualties from, 45–46
start of, 41
World War II, 53

Young Turks, 38, 39–40, 51

Zelve, 18

Picture Credits

About the Author

Chris Eboch is the author of The Well of Sacrifice, a middle-grade historical adventure set in ninth century Guatemala. Turkey is her first nonfiction book for Lucent; her second is Yemen. Eboch has visited more than twenty-five countries to indulge her love of history and travel. She studied photography at Rhode Island School of Design and writing at Emerson College. She lives in New Mexico.